Women of the Bible

Women of the Bible

FRANCES  VANDER VELDE

kregel
PUBLICATIONS

Grand Rapids, MI 49501

Women of the Bible by Frances Vander Velde

© 1957, 2000
Second Edition

Published by Kregel Publications, a division of Kregel, Inc., P.O. Box 2607, Grand Rapids, MI 49501. For more information about Kregel Publications, visit our web site: www.kregel.com

Library of Congress Cataloging-in-Publication Data
Vander Velde, Frances.
    Women of the Bible / by Frances Vander Velde.—2nd ed.
        p.   cm.
    Includes bibliographical references.
    1. Bible—Biography. 2. Women in the Bible. I. Title.
BS575 .V3   2000   220.9'2'082—dc21   00-062940
                                                        CIP
ISBN 0-8254-3964-7

Printed in the United States of America

1 2 3 4 5 / 04 03 02 01 00

Contents

Preface

The women came out of all the cities of Israel . . .
the women and the children.
—1 Samuel 18:6

 It has been my pleasure to become intimately acquainted with these women of the shrouded, mystic past, and my heart ached for them in their trials, loneliness, and pain. My spirit was led through the whole range of emotions with Hannah. The loyalty and sweetness of Ruth made many of my days serene. I was ashamed with Salome. The fragrance of Mary's spikenard distilled adoration into my own heart. I walked with the Marys in the crowd that followed the blessed Lord, and I felt the heartbreak of the Magdalene at the foot of the cross. I was sad with these women and glad with them and felt so intensely for them that I feel that I know them as well as my own sisters. It has been delightful and exciting to meet the women of the ages, long since covered with the dust and debris of earth and unreality—and to find that they were, surprisingly, much like myself.

The Bible is the story of redemption as it begins and slowly unfolds to its predetermined fulfillment. The Bible is history—each name and place and event is factual. Nothing that present-day scholars and scientists uncover from the dust of the past can, or ever will, shake the foundations of Christianity. They will only continue to prove, with startling accuracy, that the Bible is the *truth* and that God *is;* that Eve, Rebekah, Rahab, and Ruth were not mythical but were real people who filled a real place in their world and in God's plan of redemption.

In imaginatively reconstructing the lives of these wonderful women of the Word, we do not add to God's revelation but rather try to understand it better and so learn and profit the more from it. God's gift of the imagination, which takes into account the age in which these women lived, their customs and environment, and which dares to question, to challenge, and to read all things in any way pertinent to the reconstruction of the story, does not destroy faith but enlarges it.

We only have glimpses of many of these women of the Word. However, we prayerfully search the Scriptures. Pondering also the additional light that God has providentially provided in scientific research, we come to see that the women of past centuries were much like what we are, for the essence of living has changed very little. Their lives were composed of few great deeds—but rather of the commonplace, little things that make up life today. The women of the past were busy with endless housecleaning, laundry, cooking, and the multitudinous cares that children bring. Like us they coped with their emotional lives—their likes and dislikes, their frustrations and fears. The women of the Bible were all living women of flesh and blood with faults, passions, and virtues. We study their lives and feel as if we have met them and actually know them, and we find that we have much in common with them all. Sarah with her jealousy of Hagar, Leah with her heartache, Salome with her ambition for her sons, and Martha with her bustling good intentions—each woman, with her own temperament, peculiarities, and problems finds her counterpart in modern women. Because the real issues of life and the reasons for being have not changed, we can learn from them the way to happiness, peace, and faith in God. For *all* Scripture is profitable for reproof, for correction, and instruction—for right and blessed living.

I have attempted, in each brief sketch of these prominent women of the Bible, to give a character analysis rather than an exposition of the related text. This was done, however, with the hope and prayer that it would lead to a *searching* of the Scriptures rather than the perfunctory reading of the Bible that has become so common in our busy modern age. I humbly confess that these character sketches have only begun to unfold the beauty and the riches of the divine Word, and I hope that the suggestions for discussion and study at the end of each story will bring added blessings to many.

What has been done in the quiet hours, salvaged from a busy family life, has been given as to the Lord. I pray that He will graciously forgive its imperfections, in His own way fill in its limitations, and in some small measure use these humble efforts for His glory.

Acknowledgments

$\mathcal{N}$othing anyone can do of any worth at all is ever done alone. First, I thank my Lord who has led me along divers ways, always loving me and irresistibly drawing me close to Him. He is my wisdom, my strength, and my song.

To my husband, Maurice, I owe more than he will ever know. Without his encouragement and faith, the first sketch would never have been completed, nor the rest written with such pleasure and profit. I am indebted to the Reverend Arthur De Kruyter, with whom the idea for this series of studies originated, for his wise counsel and editorial contribution. I am especially indebted to Mr. George Harper of Calvin College for his expert and invaluable perusal of the entire manuscript. I am appreciative of the many friends— women especially—who have encouraged me in many ways. Last, but not least, I am grateful to my children who have shared their mother for countless hours with the wonderful women of the Word.

She shall be called Woman.
—Genesis 2:23

1

Eve

Scripture Reading
Genesis 1:26–28; 2:18–25; 3; 4:1–2, 25;
2 Corinthians 11:3; 1 Timothy 2:13–15

*I*n the beginning God created the woman . . . and behold she was very good and beautiful. She was the last and crowning act of His whole stupendous creation. She was heaven's best, last gift. When she received the breath of life, the work of Omnipotence was finished. There was nothing more to be done. God saw that all was perfect and complete, and then the "morning stars sang together, and all the sons of God shouted for joy" (Job 38:7).

The woman was called Eve, and she was the most beautiful woman in all the world of all time. She was the only one to be perfectly and personally fashioned a woman by the Creator, and the only woman whose home was Paradise. The greatest artists and poets have been able to convey only a faint idea of what Eve was like as she came from the hands of the Creator, the only being to look upon a completed world. She lacked no charm and has been pictured with celestial beauty. She was arrayed in all human perfection, radiant loveliness, perfect symmetry, and perfect intelligence.

Some of the loftiest passages in Milton's *Paradise Lost* describe Eve, who was:

> So lovely fair
> That what seemed fair in all the world seemed now
> Mean, or in her contained or in her looks
> Grace was in all her steps, heaven in her eye,
> In every gesture dignity and love.

Eve was the most interesting woman in the world because she was the first woman, the first wife, mother, and grandmother, and the mother of every living soul. Hers was the first marriage, and hers was the first joy and wonder of motherhood. She was also the first sinner—the first to feel pain, to shed tears, to see death, and to know sorrow. And mercifully, Eve was the first woman to whom salvation was promised.

In the story of Eve, we find reason for being, the beginning of misery, and the sure hope of life that is eternal, pristine in its beauty, and indescribably glorious.

The Creation of Eve

The sixth day of creation was distinguished by a double creative act, for on that day God made both the land animals and man. When He made man something special was called for. As to the rest of creation, God said, "Let there be . . . ," but when He made man, a heavenly conference is suggested for He says in Genesis 1:26, "Let *us* make man. . . ." The creation of man was so important that it called for a council of the Trinity. Man was to be the crowning creative act. He was to be created in God's image, in true knowledge, in righteousness and holiness, after His likeness, and capable of communion with his Creator. He was to be made a little lower than the angels, crowned with glory, power, and dominion. "So God created man in his own image, in the image of God created he him; male and female created he them" (Gen. 1:27). He made Eve *also* a partaker of the divine image and of dominion over all. God blessed both Adam and Eve and told them to occupy the earth with their children, to have dominion in the earth, and to use the vast resources that it contained. The first pair was vested with authority over all the works of God's hands.

Adam first exercised his authority and his discernment, as well as his power of speech, when he gave names to the animals. As he observed the creatures he saw that they were created either in swarms or in pairs. He alone was created an individual. He was above the animals in that he alone was made in God's image—with all that it implied. He was created to have spiritual communion with his Maker, but in all creation there was not found one with whom he could have physical fellowship. Not among the creatures nor in the Creator could he find his complement. Naming the animals brought to his consciousness his deep desire for human companionship: ". . . but for Adam there was not found a help meet for him" (Gen. 2:20). The Lord had a purpose in charging Adam with this task and said in response to Adam's desire and need, "It is not good that the man should be alone; I will make him a help meet for him" (Gen. 2:18).

The help God made was a woman. She was the last of God's creative acts. Adam was formed from the dust, but the woman was formed out of higher, more precious material—she was bone of his bone, flesh of his flesh. God caused Adam to fall into a deep and unusual sleep, and while he was asleep God fashioned the woman from one of his ribs. She was unique in that God made her with His own hands. She came, a perfect woman, into a perfect world—one that was ready in every way to receive her. Fashioned for and after man, woman reflects, in her human nature, the glory of man. The man is the head of the woman, but the woman is a crown to her husband (1 Cor. 11:7–12; Prov. 12:4).

The Marriage of Eve

Now God presented this perfect woman to Adam. Imagine his astonishment and joy when he woke and saw beside him this beautiful woman. God had now provided him with a partner—one who understood him and one with whom he could find fellowship. The first human love, in all its perfection, filled his heart, and he exclaimed with delight, "This is now bone of my bones, and flesh of my flesh: she shall be called Woman, because she was taken out of man" (Gen. 2:23). What heavenly benedictions must have rested upon this first pair as they stood before the Lord, clothed in innocence, perfect in beauty, joy, and love. Here we see the first marriage arranged, instituted, and blessed by God. Every marriage so effected should bring happiness. God brings men and women together today too, when they look to Him for fulfillment. The *conviction* that God brings us together is so important to happiness in marriage. Happiness is the calm confidence of *knowing* that He will make all things work together for our good.

This first marriage was more than a social or civil contract. It was not a union of convenience or of necessity. It was a perfect union, consummated in perfect love. How many marry for other reasons than that of love! How many marry without the consent or blessing of parents! Comparatively few seek God's will and blessing or make Him the silent partner in establishing this most important of human institutions and relationships. And then we wonder why so many marriages fail!

There is a beautiful song sometimes heard at weddings: "God Gave You to Me." How lightly we and our children take these precious words. Our concern is often exclusively in the elaborate affairs that our weddings have become and in the elaborate home furnishings considered so necessary today. It is essential that we teach our children, and learn for ourselves, that true happiness in marriage is not founded on material things.

The deepest happiness can be found in marriage if each finds God's gift in the other partner. The prime requisite for happiness is true love for each other. We can find no better definition for love than this: loving is giving, constant giving of oneself for and to the other. That means consideration of one another at all times. There is no surer way to happiness than that.

There is so much unhappiness in our homes because we do not show consideration of the other's feelings and desires. As women, we are often guilty in this respect—only *our* wishes and desires count. We want so many new things all the time. Keeping up with the Joneses is perhaps a fault found more often in women than in men. Many a woman wants more, materially and socially, than her husband can supply her with and becomes petulant and blaming, nagging him day after day. The basis of such an attitude is selfishness, and there is no way to kill love more quickly. Happiness is found not in getting, but in giving and giving and giving again.

If together you and your partner begin with God and you find that you have less materially than your sister or your friend, it should make no difference in the success of your marriage. Paul said, "I have learned, in whatsoever state I am, therewith to be content" (Phil. 4:11). That is a lesson we need to learn today. As parents, we are morally obligated to teach our children the principles of Christian marriage lest they, as so many do, find their marriage shipwrecked on the rocks of selfishness and discontent.

Eve was all that Adam needed for his complement—physically, intellectually, and socially. She became his partner and companion. This is what every woman should be for her husband today. She should find her counterpart in man, for that is how God willed it. God made her to be a help meet (fitting, good) for man. The man finds delight in using his strength to provide for and protect the woman, and the wife finds her place in sympathetically helping and finding fellowship with her husband.

In Genesis 2:24 we find the inspired declaration of the law of marriage. It says that the unity between the two parties must not be dissolved. That, too, should arrest our attention, for there is an increasing amount of indifference to the sacredness of marriage. We do not say, "Honor thy father and thy mother—unless they have faults." Neither should we say (or live as if we believe), "I will cleave to my husband and be loyal to him—as long as he does not hurt my feelings or is not hard to get along with."

We read that the first pair were clothed in innocence, and as such they were also an example for posterity. Our bodies are temples of the Holy Spirit, and we should keep them pure and clean. As Christian parents, we should stay aware of moral issues. Innocence is outmoded today. We should teach our children to live morally clean lives, that it is important to start marriage with a clean record.

The Temptation of Eve

One beautiful day, tragedy struck the garden of Eden. The pristine beauty and purity of the first pair was shattered. Their robes of innocence fell away, leaving only the nakedness of sin. At the center of this catastrophe was the lovely woman whom God had given to delight and help man.

Man and woman had been created morally responsible beings with a free will to serve their Lord. This the Evil Tempter knew, and he entered the garden to try them. Now Satan, the general of hades, carefully planned his strategy. He chose the serpent, who was the most subtle of all the creatures, for his medium. Next, he chose his approach, not through Adam, who was the legal head of the human race, but through Eve, the partner. Did he choose her because she was the weaker of the two? Did he think she would be easier to deceive, or was she the more ambitious of the two? Was Satan seeking the fall of man through man's helper?

The Prince of Evil is superb in strategy. He chose a time that was favorable, when Eve was alone and within sight of the forbidden tree. Although Eve had no reason to fear the serpent, we are amazed at the freedom with which she discussed such an important matter with this creature. We see in the ensuing conversation how diabolically clever Satan was. He did not tell Eve to disobey but led her on by subtle suggestion. He said, in effect, "Yea, hath God said—but *has He really?* I would never believe He would deny you anything!" So he led her to suspect the divine goodness and endeavored to shake her confidence in God. She should have turned away, for there is always danger in arguing with evil. In Genesis 3:2–3, she told him that she might eat from every tree but one and that there was a stern penalty for disobeying. She looked and listened intently as the Father of Lies told her, "Do not believe that at all. Look at the fruit—does it look bad? Why, it is just as fine as any other. God is not telling you the truth. Don't believe for a moment that you will die if you eat it." With this argument, he tried to make Eve disbelieve the divine Word and to remove her fear of punishment. Finally, inciting competitive thoughts, Satan whispered that God had a secret motive—a fear of rivalry! For the truth was, he insisted, that if she ate of this fruit she would be as God—she would know *everything.*

Eve listened too long. This subtle yielding to sin's suggestion had already begun to alienate her heart from God. She had everything she needed for true happiness, and the tree of life could have maintained this for her. But she looked and found something different here—something alluring—and the awful climax came as she reached for the fruit and ate it. She not only fell from grace but became the temptress herself. She enticed her husband to eat with her.

To invite companionship in the enjoyment of questionable pleasures is the very nature of sin. Adam also ate of the forbidden fruit and so joined Eve in sin. The Arch Deceiver had perpetrated his evil design. He brought ruin to the world that God made and called good. We can almost see the Old Serpent gloat as he slunk away through the trees—his mission accomplished!

It is good for us to study the psychology of the first temptation. The Serpent's approach to Eve, by way of subtle suggestion, worked so well that he has used it ever since. He still says that sin is nothing to worry about, that everyone does it and that God is too loving to punish it.

The core of Eve's sin was selfishness. So much of sin is selfishness. We can find so many good reasons for taking all we can get for ourselves. What we can get is so often uppermost in our minds— instead of what we can do for others. Jesus said, "Whosoever will come after me, let him deny himself" (Mark 8:34). But the Devil says, "Don't believe that. The way to get ahead, and stay ahead, is to think of yourself first." And how we talk along with him!

The immediate result of sin in the first pair was a sense of guilt. Their first act was to hide from God. Sin always drives a wedge of guilt between us and God. It was an awful and solemn moment when God came to fallen man and woman with the question, "Where art thou? . . . Hast thou eaten of the tree?" (Gen. 3:9, 11). But instead of confessing, which is the way to peace, they blamed each other for their sin. And how often we do the same thing today! We blame others for leading us into wrong. We find excuses for our actions. We blame our dispositions, our circumstances, and generally defend ourselves for the wrong we do and the heartache we cause.

Though there is pardon for sin, there is no excuse for it. Adam and Eve stood before God in all the ugliness of guilt, and the Supreme Judge had to mete out His sentence. The serpent was cursed for his part in the first transgression. Even though Eve's was the first sin, Adam was held more responsible, for as legal head of the human race he had plunged all posterity into the misery and degradation of sin. Making a livelihood would no longer be pure pleasure but would become a continual struggle with the elements and with the ground that was cursed for his sake.

We are interested primarily in the consequences of sin for Eve. The sentence pronounced on her related chiefly to her position as wife and mother. From then on her desire would be for her husband, and he would rule over her. From the beginning she was meant to have children, but she would now have to bear them in extreme anguish and sorrow.

When her first son, Cain, was born, Adam named his wife Eve, because she was the mother of all living. After this, Abel was born and, later, Seth. Then we read that all through the long life Eve lived with Adam she had many sons and daughters. We know from subsequent history that not only did she suffer bringing her children into the world but her grief and sorrow were multiplied in the problems and sin of her children. There was consolation for Eve, however, for there was the promise of the One who would conquer all evil and bring His redeemed to a new Paradise.

The story of Eve is so old, it is as old as history itself—but the more we think about it the more certain we become that it contains many and valuable lessons to guide us in this modern world.

Suggestions for Discussion

1. Is there any significance in the fact that God created land animals and man on the same day?
2. Do you think God had a purpose in creating Eve in a different way from Adam?
3. What does it mean that woman is a crown to her husband?
4. What does the word "woman" mean?
5. How does this first marriage differ from those of today?
6. Many married people today consider divorce if they do not find happiness together. Do you think that this is the best course?
7. What is the best solution to serious marital problems: engaging a psychiatrist, consulting a minister, discussing it with the family or friends, or seeking God's help through prayer? Why?
8. Do you think that frankness about sex is more conducive to clean living than the reticence of former years?
9. Why do you think that Satan chose to tempt Eve first?
10. How many different names can you find for Satan in the Bible?
11. What would you say was the impelling motive for Eve's sin?
12. What were the immediate results of Eve's sin for herself? For us?

Sarah obeyed Abraham, calling him lord: whose daughters ye are, as long as ye do well.
—1 Peter 3:6

2

Sarah

Scripture Reading
Genesis 17:15–21; 18:1–15; 21:1–8;
1 Peter 3:1–7

The story of the life and times of Sarah is interesting and impressive. Her life is a wonderful testimony to the marvelous grace of God. Her life was one with her husband Abraham as he became, through trial, testing, and divine favor, the father of the faithful and, in a unique way, the friend of God.

To gain the greatest profit from any character study, we should not limit our Scripture reading to the few verses in which the person is specifically mentioned. If we want to know all about Sarah and her famous husband, we should read every chapter from Genesis 12 to 24 and all other references to them in the Scriptures. Reading these twelve chapters will take no more time than it takes to read a magazine article, and it will be far more rewarding.

There are so many good books to read and magazines to choose from. Not all we read is worth our precious time, however, and we must give thought to choosing the best. The Bible is the best book.

It is *always,* and in *every way,* profitable to read. Notwithstanding, the open Bible is a closed book in many of our homes. "Read the Bible Sunday," which is observed in many churches, is an admission of how often Christian people neglect their Bible reading. It will take much prayer, consecration, and determination to transfer some of the zeal for secular reading to sacred reading. A study of the life of Sarah will delight you and increase your desire for the Word.

Parents also should be aware of what their children read, for they are developing reading habits that will not be easily broken. We want them to appreciate and read good literature but not to neglect the Bible. What shall it profit young people if they gain a whole world of knowledge and lose their own souls?

Sarai at Home

The life of the blessed woman who became the mother of nations began in a heathen environment. Her father-in-law, Terah, a descendant of Shem, must have remembered the traditions of the flood and the astounding story of Babel as well as if they had happened yesterday. Only a few hundred years had passed and again the world was desperately wicked. Even though Terah worshiped idols, God chose to break the silence of the centuries by appearing to a member of his family. The Lord chose Abram and Sarai to preserve his covenant people. Addressing Abram, Jehovah said, "Get thee out of thy country, and from thy kindred, and from thy father's house, unto a land that I will show thee: and I will make of thee a great nation, and I will bless thee, and make thy name great; and thou shalt be a blessing" (Gen. 12:1–2). And we read simply this, "So Abram departed . . . and Abram took Sarai his wife" (Gen. 12:4–5). Together they left Ur, with all its familiar scenes and faces, and never returned.

What a day it must have been for Sarai when she left. Imagine the busy preparations for what might very well be a long journey, the gathering of belongings, of herds, and of servants. Think of the excitement and the comments of the clan as they gathered around to say good-bye, the fond farewells of friends and the tumult of Sarai's own hopes and fears as they started on their pilgrim journey. With destiny unknown, Sarai and Abram stepped over the threshold of an idolatrous age into a new era. It was a good thing they were upheld by the rod and staff of God's promise, for life was to be no bed of roses for either one of them. Not knowing their destination they journeyed on, happily anticipating the promised blessings. When at last they reached Canaan, we can be sure that it was a severe test of faith that they found the new and better country already occupied, and as they looked out over the parched and famine-stricken fields there must have been fear and alarm in their hearts.

Sarai in a Harem

After Abram pondered the precarious situation in Canaan, he heard that there was corn in Egypt and decided to go there. A few centuries later, the family of his grandson trekked the same anxious path to escape another famine. For both, the way to plenty became the way to trial and testing. For Abram and Sarai, it was a trial of their own making, for they did not consult Jehovah but relied instead on their own plan.

As they traveled on, Abram looked searchingly at the lovely Sarai by his side, and fear began to gnaw at his heart. Although she was already about sixty-five years of age, she was exceptionally beautiful and carried with her an air of royal grace. Unlike the dusky Egyptians, she was fair of skin and would be sure to attract attention—too much maybe! Abram loved her with all his heart, and he may often have called her "my Princess," for that is what her name meant. So together they decided on a subterfuge. He suggested a lie for protection—and she was to tell it. His fear, however, was not for Sarai. He was especially thinking of how he might save his own skin (Gen. 12:13). Read the story in Genesis 12 and see how the very thing that they wished to avoid came to pass. Sarai was seen, admired, and taken into Pharaoh's harem. Meanwhile, Abram accepted valuable gifts from the king as a sort of dowry to a brother.

We wonder how Sarai felt as she contemplated her situation in this heathen harem. Did Abram really love her? Had he not selfishly placed his own safety and that of his herds above the risk to her chastity? Sarai was in a predicament. The deceit was discovered when God graciously intervened. The Pharaoh's house fell under a plague, and Abram the man of God stood shamefaced as he was reproved by a heathen monarch. Later Sarai found herself in a similar situation when King Abimelech took her into his harem. Again, Abram considered his own safety first, and the same kind of lie (Gen. 20:2) led to trouble and shame.

How often we find it convenient to tell a lie or a half-truth as Abram did or to consort with the world for profit. We learn from Sarai's story that a lie is never a protection but, instead, leads to serious trouble with both God and man. How wonderful it is to know that God graciously intervenes even today when His own suffer, even though it may be through the foolishness of their own ways.

Sarah in Her Tent

Sarah's greatest trial of faith went on in her camel's hair tent. There the trial of patience was long and painful. What agony of suspense she endured as she waited year after year for the heir God had promised to her and to Abram. How the sight of every newborn babe must have intensified the longing in her own heart. How much love waited to be given as her whole being reached out in anticipation of the son whom the Lord had promised so many times. Was she to be denied the one thing she wanted most of all? It seemed that all her life she had lived on promises.

Then, when faith ebbed low, Sarah thought of how God had promised them children when they left Ur and of how later God had enlarged his promise under the stars (Gen. 15:1–6)—but the promise had been made to *Abram*. "Perhaps it is to be his son, not mine," she thought. So one fateful day she ran ahead of the Lord and gave Hagar, her maid, to Abram that he might have a child. (Oh Sarah, to what trouble you opened the door! You did not anticipate the scorn of Hagar as she looked down on you, for it was she, the maid, and not you, the princess, who appeared to carry the child of promise. Your jealousy burned like a flame in your heart and drove you to meanness, to the shame of turning away a destitute one whom you wronged.) Nevertheless, Abram, sympathetic and loving, was loyal to Sarai. Best of all, the promise was still hers. It was her faith that failed, not God's promise.

Ishmael was thirteen years old when God came to Abraham again and told him that Sarai's name should now be changed to Sarah. Abraham laughed with joy when God said, "Sarah thy wife shall bear thee a son . . . and thou shalt call his name Isaac" (Gen. 17:19). His laugh was unlike the incredulous laugh of Sarah as she listened to the heavenly visitors from behind the door of her tent. She was ashamed in a moment when Jehovah asked, "Is any thing too hard for the LORD?" (Gen. 18:14). And this promise has been the strength in crisis of God's people ever since.

Twenty-five years after the first theophany, the promised son was born to Sarah. Sarah was now about ninety years old and, humanly speaking, past the age of bearing children. It was divine grace and power alone that brought the joy, light, and laughter of little Isaac into her life.

Faith had triumphed, and there was happiness in the tent of Sarah. As it became apparent that Isaac, not Ishmael, was the promised heir, new problems developed. Hagar and Ishmael were sent away, but that is another story. So we see that faith, though tested and tried, is rewarded, and Sarah is one of only two women named in the long list of the heroes of faith in Hebrews 11. Sarah, princess of many and mother of nations, is among the cloud of witnesses whose faith we emulate. We can learn from her faults and her virtues how to live a Christian life. In all her long pilgrimage, with its constant trials and testings, she loved her husband, acquiesced in his wishes, and loyally went with him who had no abiding city. She respected his high calling and was a joint heir with him of the grace of life.

Suggestions for Discussion

1. Who went with Abram and Sarai as far as Haran? Did Abram and Sarai hear from these people again. See Genesis 22:20–24.

2. What kind of separation are we, as Abram and Sarai's spiritual family, called to? If we compare our lives with those of our unsaved neighbors, how much separation can we see?

3. Do you think it was easy for Sarai to follow Abram wherever God sent him? Explain.

4. Should Abram and Sarai have stayed in Canaan and expected the Lord to provide for them in spite of famine?

5. What is a half-truth? Is a half-truth permissible for protection? When trying to evade an argument? For convenience?

6. Name three possible reasons Sarai may have had for giving Hagar to Abraham.

7. Both Abraham and Sarah laughed when they were promised a son, because they were past the proper age. Explain the difference in the laughter of each.

8. Did Sarah's attitude toward Ishmael indicate spiritual insight or jealousy?

9. In what ways were the circumstances surrounding Christ's and Isaac's births similar?

10. What do we know about Sarah's death?

11. How is Sarah an example to us?

Remember Lot's wife.
—Luke 17:32

3

Lot's Wife

Scripture Reading
Genesis 13; 19

$\mathscr{A}$lways the severest critic of woman is woman," says a certain writer. He goes on to say: "Men are inclined to be lenient and generous with women. Though men tend to like each other, women are not so quick to like one another. They do not so readily believe each other and are often quick to criticize." Think about this—is it true? An honest self-analysis may be both necessary and profitable.

Perhaps, if we cannot say something kind or good about another woman, it would be better not to say anything at all. However, our failure to say an appreciative word or pay an occasional compliment does not necessarily imply that there is nothing good to be said. It could be pride, or envy, or simply preoccupation with self that accounts for the critical attitude of a woman toward another woman.

Lot's wife, however, is a woman about whom we hear nothing at all but criticism. In all of your life, have you ever heard a kind word about her? Yet those who knew her best might have said it was a pity that a woman as nice and as likable as Lot's wife should be destroyed.

Her Spiritual Inheritance

She has been called by some the Mayor's wife or the Frozen Face, by others Mrs. Lot or simply Lot's wife, and by everyone—a foolish woman. Never, anywhere, do we read of her love, kindness, or faith. She was neither a good wife nor a good mother. We wonder why Moses gave such a large place to her and her husband in the book that he authored. There is nothing uplifting or inspiring in the entire narrative. It calls only for censure and sadness.

When Jesus read this story, He found in it a lesson needful for the people of His day. He said to them, "Remember Lot's wife" (Luke 17:32). The story is as modern as it is ancient, for we will always find her parallel in women everywhere. Every part of the narrative indicates lessons of supreme importance, and we will do well to follow the suggestion made by our Lord to "remember Lot's wife."

Lot and his wife could not have had a better beginning or foundation on which to build a good and happy life. They were closely related to the best man on earth. Uncle Abraham was one of the world's truly great men. The important people of his day respected him for his sterling character and good influence. The fine examples of the pious and godly Abraham and Sarah were the only major influences in the lives of Lot and his wife for many years. When the call came to Abraham, they too were inspired to join the caravan, leaving all that was dear and familiar in the old country, Ur of the Chaldees. Together they traveled with flocks, herds, and servants on the divinely directed pilgrimage to Canaan. They also traveled to Egypt and back again to Canaan with a chastened and consecrated uncle. It is only reasonable to suppose that Lot's wife believed in the God of Abraham. Without a doubt, she worshiped at the altar Abraham built or at one of her own. She belonged to that select group of people who gave to the world its greatest prophets and its only Savior. Close association with the godly is always protection against evil, and if Lot and his wife had maintained that throughout their lives they would also have been numbered among the faithful.

The family of Lot realized they had the favor and blessing of God, but they did not see that their spiritual lives were enlarged because of their close association with Abraham, the father of the faithful, the friend of God. Neither did it occur to them that the rich material blessings of Abraham overflowed into their pastures, corrals, and tents. Lot's family was blessed with faithful Abraham, and it still works the same way today—many are the blessings that come from fellowship with God's people. Worshiping at the same altar with Christian parents or attending church, chiefly because of Christian influence, is all that many young people have today. But, even though there is no real consecration, there is no better thing to do than to follow the good example of Christian parents. Even after Lot and his wife chose to leave the safety of a godly atmosphere and move into the dangers of the big city, the prayers and loving concern of Abraham went with them.

Her Worldly Riches

Lot and his wife thought that they were well off materially because of their own business acumen. When a chance came to better themselves, they took it. They had, perhaps, been influenced by the prosperity that they saw in Egypt and had remembered the fertile Nile valley as they shifted their flocks from valley to hill to valley again, always in search of pasturage and water. The servants must have known that Lot was selfish, for they quarreled with Abraham's servants over the best places and took what they could. Abraham had learned not to set his heart on material things, though he had much. He preferred to part than quarrel. He generously suggested that the land be divided and that Lot choose first. This was Lot's chance to get ahead. Consideration for Abraham was abruptly shelved, and apparently, without even a thank you, Lot looked across the promised land with calculating, hard, shrewd eyes. "I have to watch out for myself, opportunity knocks but once," thought Lot, and he chose the very best he saw.

Now there is nothing unusual about choosing. We do it every day among seemingly unimportant things. We choose what we eat and wear, spend, save, or give away. We choose how we will spend our time and energy. We all must choose, at times, between things of great importance, such as courses in school, a profession, going into business, moving away, or selecting friends. We should never be too busy to notice which way our children are pitching their tents. When our boys and girls make life's greatest choices, let us be there to counsel them rather than let them go their own way only to count the cost later. For instance, when our children come to choose their life's work, we should, with them, look over the temptations and dangers that may be involved and the kind of friends that they will make.

Lot's fault was not so much that he chose the best, but that his motivation was wrong. In this case, his motivation was selfishness. He neglected to think of the spiritual needs of his family and looked only for worldly gain. Naturally, like Lot, we choose what looks the best to us. And we usually choose with about as much attention to real values as Lot did! Jesus was concerned about *us* when he said, "Remember Lot's wife."

Our problem in this materialistic age is the same as Lot's—a distorted sense of values. We all too often count success by the things we own. The Lots knew that Sodom was an exceedingly wicked city, but they moved there anyway and settled down to manage their extensive business affairs, for they were very rich. If increasing their wealth meant rubbing elbows and doing business with scoffers, they did it. They could stand on their own feet. Certainly they could take care of themselves. How familiar such reasoning sounds!

Her Ultimate Poverty

We read that the open and avowed wickedness of Sodom was of the basest kind (see Gen. 19:4–9; 2 Peter 2:6–10; Jude 7). Not only did Lot's wife move into Sodom but, disgustingly sinful as it was, she fell in love with it. The smoke from its chimneys hid the face of God from view, but she happily walked its streets and made friends in the marketplace, took pride in its worldly culture, and enjoyed her permanent home and prosperity. She thought she had everything.

Her husband did not like it so well. At heart, he was a good man, and he was vexed, irritated, and driven almost to distraction by what he saw and heard all around him. He knew it was wrong to have fellowship with such wicked people, but he did not have the moral strength or backbone to leave. "A double-minded man is unstable in all his ways" (James 1:8), and it is uncomfortable to limp constantly between two opinions. His wife must have known that he was distressed, and she could have been a real helper to him by urging him to take the family back to Bethel and to the God who gives peace. Let us pray that our influence in the home may always be for good and for God!

Think of the daughters of Lot's wife who could never call their mother blessed and whose last memorial of her was that of a frozen face with a backward look. They missed the love and the guidance that only a Christian mother can give. Is that why they loved the glitter and glamour of the world and ate, drank, and were merry with their sinful Sodomite friends? Though Lot's wife must have loved her daughters dearly, the only heritage she left them was a distorted sense of moral values, a material and spiritual poverty. They had no home.

When Lot's wife was told of the impending doom of the city she loved, she believed it but, having a divided heart, she lingered. (A divided heart is a wretched heart, and indecision is crippling to a vital Christian life. We cannot set our hearts both on riches and on God: "Ye cannot serve God and mammon" [Matt. 6:24].) The angel had to take her hand and urge her out of the city. However, instead of hurrying along, thankful to be spared such an awful fate, she looked back longingly at the city, for her heart was still there. This was disobedience to the divine command (Gen. 19:17), and she became a pillar of salt. Transfixed in her backward look, she became a monumental warning to all who love the world and the things of the world. In her passion for possession, she lost all—everything she owned, her spiritual inheritance, and her immortal soul. And you and I, who remember Lot's wife, can only humbly say, "There but for the grace of God, stand I."

Suggestions for Discussion

1. What are some of the benefits that Lot and his wife received in their association with Abraham and Sarah?
2. How far did the family of Lot travel with Abraham and Sarah?
3. Do you think that it is a good thing to take our children to church with us even if they seem not to derive much benefit from the services? Why?
4. Is it always better to part than to quarrel?
5. What does the Bible have to say about the inordinate desire for possessions? See Luke 12:15; Ephesians 5:3; Colossians 3:5; and Hebrews 13:5.
6. Can you explain the attraction of Sodom for Lot's wife?
7. How do we know that her daughters grew up with a distorted sense of values?
8. What kind of influence did she exert on her husband?
9. How do we know Lot was basically a good man?
10. Find references in the Bible to Sodom and Gomorrah. What does the destruction of these cities typify?

What aileth thee, Hagar? Fear not; for God hath heard. . . .
—Genesis 21:17

4

Hagar

Scripture Reading
Genesis 16; 21:1–21

The strength of a nation is directly related to the condition of its homes. This is a recognized truth. A tremendous responsibility lies with women, for it is the hand that rocks the cradle that rules the world. The influence of the mother in molding the character and, in part, the destiny of the child far outweighs any other influence.

There is alarm over the increasing number of broken homes due to divorce in America, the land of brotherhood and great opportunities. And, if the glory of a nation is rooted in well-adjusted and integrated families, none of us should be complacent about this problem but should give it serious thought and a large place in our prayers.

Families are often broken up by death, divorce, and the separation of their members. It is well known that juvenile delinquency is caused by the disruption of families in our social structure. If the family is the basic unit of society, it follows that our social structure falls when homes disintegrate.

Yet, special studies have revealed that almost as many juvenile delinquents come from homes that are intact but in which there are emotional conflicts, tensions, and attitudes that precipitate family disorganization. Such homes are as surely broken and morally shattered as openly divorced ones. Notice how often a delinquent or criminal will blame their social maladjustment to the continual quarreling of their parents. A study of the life of Hagar, who lived in a home in which there were serious family problems, will prove once again that all Scripture is given for reproof, correction, and instruction for right and blessed living.

Hagar the Girl

The tale of Hagar, the slave girl who became her wealthy master's wife and the mother of his son, sounds like a rags-to-riches story. But instead of having a happy sequence, it is a story of bitterness and heartache, of dreams turned to ashes, of a fountain of tears. It is a most pathetic story, typical in some ways of the unhappy family conditions that we have today.

Hagar had not come from Ur with Sarah but was an Egyptian girl. Sarah had spent some time in Egypt and, while there, likely found she had need of a maid. She heard of Hagar, tried her, and found that she had the necessary qualifications. The little girl was capable, obedient, and trustworthy. Sarah was rich and influential, and Hagar's family may have had little choice in the matter. So Hagar was taken from her mother's home and traveled hundreds of miles, through the heat and winds of the desert, to a far country. She became the property or slave girl of the princess. She must have served her mistress with a devotion intensified by feelings of loneliness, for she had been separated from all the things that were familiar and dear to her. She was far from home now that she was living in Canaan, and Sarah had to be mother as well as mistress to the poor Egyptian girl. Hagar must have loved and admired the beautiful and gracious Sarah. She was fortunate indeed to be a slave in such a noble and good family.

Hagar occupied an important place in the small and intimate family circle. In her close association with Sarah, she soon learned about her God. She was told that the idols of the Egyptians were not gods at all and that there was only one true God. He it was that made the sky with its stars, the sand by the seashore, the green fields, and the cattle upon a thousand hills. That this great God had made Abraham his very special friend filled Hagar with great respect and veneration for her master.

She soon heard about the son whom God had promised to give. Indeed, Abraham and Sarah could talk of little else—sometimes with assurance, sometimes with doubt, *always* with longing. This son of promise was to be a man of destiny. He was to inherit all the promises given to Abraham, and in him all the families of the earth would be blessed. She soon discovered that this one great dream gave point and enthusiasm to their lives. What a privilege it was for Hagar to share that dream. She, unlike the other servants, would be near the wonderful child—perhaps she could care for it! As the years passed, she looked forward to the day when Sarah would be completely happy and Abraham would be the proud father of the promised heir.

But for Sarah, these ten years that Hagar was with her were desperate with waiting and longing. Like any normal Eastern woman, she was ashamed of her sterility. She was getting along in years, and with her fading beauty went her rosy dreams. She thought of acquiring a child through her maid, Hagar, and talked it over with her husband. To have a secondary wife was socially accepted in those days, and Sarah's motive was good. She was to relinquish unselfishly her dearest dream. It took humility to allow another woman the honor of being the mother of the son she had once claimed by faith.

With pity and tenderness for Sarah, Abraham agreed to the plan to take Hagar for the purpose of having a child. But, however noble Sarah's attitude appeared, both she and Abraham sinned—to take another wife was a clear violation of God's law (Gen. 2:24). Also, Sarah was placing a dangerous temptation in her husband's way. It was also wrong because, though Hagar was her bondwoman, Sarah had no right to use her in this way and without her consent. In both, there was lack of faith. Together they arranged to take for themselves the child that God had promised to give.

How like them we are! How often we plan and take without praying and asking God for wisdom and guidance. Afterward, we piously thank the Lord for what we have procured for ourselves. Often our choices lead to unhappy predicaments out of which the Lord must graciously help us. We all must learn to pray and wait.

Hagar the Wife

After the two had agreed on a more practical way to proceed than waiting, Sarah called in Hagar and gave her to Abraham, and he took her to be his wife. Here began the marital triangle that was to shatter the peace of this pious family.

For Hagar, the unexpected elevation from servant to master's wife was most amazing. With understandable pride she stood beside him as his other wife. Imagine her elation when she found that she was going to have a child. Now she scorned to bend her proud head to tie the sandals on the feet of her mistress. Perhaps she had vain dreams of taking Sarah's place as the favored woman. It was apparent that she was to bring the precious heir into the world, and she expected every consideration.

Sarah had expected no rival in the humble slave, or she would never have made her such an intimate member of the family circle. She was stung with remorse and bitter jealousy as, day by day, she saw the proud bearing of Hagar with whom she had shared Abraham's love and attention. That Hagar, unexpectedly taken out of her lowly station and admitted to the high privilege of being the master's wife, became high-minded is to be understood. She could not have fully grasped the reasons and the motive of Abraham, nor the changed attitude of Sarah.

Sarah had sown seed for a family feud, and now she was reaping what she had sown. She had created a situation that was too involved for her to cope with. The pain of childlessness was nothing compared to the wild tumult in her heart now. Sarah found she could no longer stand the insolence of Hagar, and in anger and frustration she bitterly complained to Abraham (Gen. 16:5). Abraham was the slave of circumstances and had to make the best of a painful situation. Even though Hagar had strong claims on Abraham's consideration and regard, he told Sarah, "Do to her as it pleaseth thee" (Gen. 16:6). So Sarah took out her remorse on Hagar by pressing her tired back hard to menial tasks. What a reflection on Sarah, who owed her nothing but consideration!

Hurt and bewildered, Hagar fled into the wilderness toward Egypt where the angel of the Lord found her, worn and dejected, by a stream. In the heart of her mistress there was hatred, but the angel gave her pity and the promise of a son, whom she was to call Ishmael. He promised her great blessings but reminded her that she was still a servant and had to return and be obedient to her mistress. With a consciousness that God saw and watched over her, she returned to Sarah.

The son of Abraham and Hagar was born and, following the command of the angel, Abraham called him Ishmael. Though the unhappy circumstances surrounding the coming of Ishmael had tremendously disturbed the domestic scene, Abraham now had his son. How pleased he was! How he loved him and tried to teach him the fear of the Lord. Try to see the tender father-and-son comradeship that grew between them and the close relationship of sharing the wondrous promises of God.

After thirteen happy years together, the Lord came to talk with Abraham again. Abraham was baffled by the news that Ishmael was not the promised seed, and he prayed the Lord, "O that Ishmael might live before thee!" (Gen. 17:18). But God answered, "Sarah thy wife shall bear thee a son indeed; and thou shalt call his name Isaac: and I will establish my covenant with *him*" (Gen. 17:19, emphasis added).

Hagar the Outcast

As the curtain rises on the third act of the sad drama of the life of Hagar, we look out upon a desolate scene. The hot sands of the desert stretched as far as the eye can see. The burning winds drew fingers across the sands, etching endless lines that led to nowhere. There was not a tree in sight and no water to relieve the agonizing thirst of those caught in the scorching desert sun. The sharp sand stung Hagar with a thousand needles as she lay, lost and helpless, in the white heat, which had brought the agony of thirst. Beyond her somewhat, beneath a shriveled shrub, her precious son lay dying of thirst. There was the quiet of death until, suddenly, the soundless desert was pierced with a cry of distress. Between the uncontrollable sobs, which tore her weary body, she heard a voice. It was a ministering angel who asked, "What aileth thee, Hagar?" (Gen. 21:17).

※　　　※　　　※

Hagar and her son, Ishmael, were outcasts! What a dramatic story was hers. Abraham's promised and long-awaited heir had been born to Sarah in her old age, amidst great rejoicing. How disturbing to the mind of Ishmael had been the increasing popularity of Isaac! How little could the youth understand the change in his, heretofore, favored circumstances. Now, it was little Isaac who received the attention and adoration of all. It was Isaac who was the center of attraction, and Ishmael, who had long been pampered, did what many another child would have done—he taunted and teased Isaac, which so irritated and exasperated Sarah that she told Abraham to cast out the bondwoman and her son. Sarah's sin was still bearing fruit, causing disintegration in the home and trouble with the children.

There is a lesson of another kind that we should learn from this. How different the home life would have been if Ishmael had been disciplined and taught to have respect and consideration for others in his family. A child's first encounter with the law is in the home.

Delinquency is not necessarily running away from home or holding up a filling station. Its seeds are sown in early life in disrespect and disobedience to parents. It is the task of every parent to teach children consideration for others, to require obedience, and to exercise authority. Consideration for others would have kept Ishmael and Hagar, who failed to discipline her son, safe at home. Yet, in it all, we must not forget that Hagar was more sinned against than sinning.

There was mercy in the visit of the angel. Hagar was a specially blessed woman, for this was the second time that the angel of the Lord had come to her aid. Of what other woman can this be said? He showed her springs of water, and she and her son drank and lived. He followed her with a blessing and made of her son a great, strong nation.

Today, if we will but hear His voice, God still calls the weary, the burdened, and the outcast to come to Him. They who come to Him He will in no wise cast out (John 6:37) but will give them living waters to drink, and they will never thirst again. And for those who say in faith, "Thou God seest me" (Gen. 16:13), there shall one day be no more sorrow, for God shall wipe away all tears from their eyes.

Suggestions for Discussion

1. Was it humility or pride that led Sarah to give Hagar to be Abraham's wife?
2. Define the following terms: polygamy, polygyny, and polyandry.
3. Why do you suppose God waited so long to give Sarah the child He had promised?
4. Explain Hagar's changed attitude after she became Abraham's wife.

5. Does the fact that Hagar recognized the angel of the Lord tell us anything about her religious training or her faith (Gen. 16:7–14)?

6. Did the angel of the Lord reveal Hagar's true relationship to Abraham and Sarah? Explain.

7. How did Abraham feel about sending Ishmael away?

8. What promise did God make to Abraham regarding Ishmael? See Genesis 17:20. To Hagar? See Genesis 16:10–12 and 21:18.

9. Why do you think Hagar sat some distance from Ishmael in the desert?

10. What do we know about Ishmael's later life?

11. Compare the status of the two sons of Abraham. What are the spiritual implications? See Galatians 4:22–31.

12. What is the difference between mocking and teasing? How much teasing should we allow among our children?

And Isaac loved Esau, . . . but Rebekah loved Jacob.
—Genesis 25:28

5

Rebekah

Scripture Reading
Genesis 24; 25:19–28; 27; 28:1–9

$\mathcal{S}$econd on the list of the most important decisions in life is that of choosing a marriage partner. Choosing to
serve the Lord comes first.

It is no accident that God gave children into the charge of parents for a score or more years, and conscientious parents are concerned with the well-being of their children from infancy through
maturity. They face the constant problems of providing good food
and proper rest for them all through the growing years. They try to
provide the best possible education for their children so that eventually they may earn a good livelihood. Parents do all they can to
foster good feelings and a sense of fair play in children, to mold
their characters so that they may be socially well-adjusted.

Finally, the time arrives when children go out from the protective home environment and choose the friends among whom they
will eventually find partners for the most serious adventure of their
lives. Their judgment may not be as mature as it appears, and they
will still need the unflagging interest of those who love them most.

Too often, at this period, the biggest problem appears to be obtaining the keys to the family car—and the money to spend.

Abraham realized how hard it is for a man to be loyal to his faith when he does not have the backing of a good wife. He wanted no pagan wife for Isaac, and he did something about it. He made it a matter of prayer. He also saw to it that Isaac would meet the right kind of girl. We can and should do exactly that. It is no surprise that God answers such prayers. This He has always done. And we can encourage our children to go where they will meet their kind, too. How interested are mothers in having their girls or boys in Christian young people's groups in your church and city? The influence of years of Christian training should be such that your youth will want to be with others of like belief.

Don't wait until your son or daughter brings home an unbeliever. All your criticism and pleading will not help, for then it will be too late. Prayer and guidance come first, and if they do, God will answer with the abundant blessing of happy homes and hearts.

Romance

The sun is going down in royal splendor as Eliezar approaches the little eastern town of Haran in Syria. He has come from the south, has been traveling for days, and is glad to dismount by the well outside the city. His dusty riders climb down from the camels that kneel in the warm sand. It is divine providence that he and his ten thirsty camels have come here at the close of the day, but it is the wisdom of the shrewd old servant that causes him to rest beside the well. He knows that the women and girls of the city will be here without fail to get water for their families' evening use.

The girls make a pretty picture as they come gaily talking and laughing down the path. Like a portrait against a sky-curtain of rose and mauve and gold, they slowly saunter, pitchers held high on their shoulders. Their *malaayas* swish softly as they approach with youthful grace.

No sooner does Eliezar, Abraham's most trusted servant, see them, than he bows his head in prayer. Simply and directly he prays to God for help. (It is obvious from his retinue that he serves an important man. Eliezar has never before been sent on such an important mission. He has come to find, and bring back with him, a suitable wife for the young prince. Abraham has impressed him with the seriousness of making the proper choice.) Eliezar of Damascus is still praying as Rebekah comes near. Though she has no inkling of it, he opens his eyes to see the answer to his prayer.

As he sees Rebekah step down to fill her pitcher, he is struck by her loveliness. He hurries toward her and asks for a drink. She is polite and poised, gracious and generous. Eliezar is impressed by her eagerness and enthusiasm as she offers to water his camels also. Stirred as he is by her beauty, he is even more stirred by her beautiful character. Out of his saddlebags he brings gifts, and he asks her name. He is pleased with the frankness and hospitality of Bethuel's daughter and immediately gives God thanks. He is sure he has found the ideal woman, the heaven-appointed bride! How winsome she is as she runs, first of all, to her mother's house to tell of the visitor come from great-uncle Abraham. (How ideal it is for a girl to go to mother with all her confidences. There is no safer place for secrets, no happier place for joys, than in a mother's heart.)

Eliezar was entertained in royal Eastern fashion at the house of Bethuel, Abraham's nephew. With what rapt attention they listened to all he had to tell of Abraham's prosperity, and of Sarah and Isaac! Breathlessly, they listened to Eliezar speak of his prayer and God's answer. Soberly, they looked at one another and said, "The thing proceedeth from the LORD" (Gen. 24:50).

It was a young woman of decision and courage who said, "I will go" (Gen. 24:58). God had promised to bless all nations through Abraham's family, she was told, and it was with mixed emotions of faith, the love of adventure and romance, and the thought of wealth and prestige that she hurriedly prepared to go with the trusted servant, Eliezar.

As the camel train once more headed south, it carried vivacious and charming Rebekah, along with her maids, to the well at Lahairoi.

The first glimpse she had of her intended husband was picturesque and bode well for the future. In the soft dusk of evening, with sheep folded and day's work done, he was found alone in the fields with God. As the soft starlight fell on his eager face, Rebekah slipped quickly from the camels to meet him. To look at Rebekah was to love her, and she became his wife.

Shadows

Rebekah soon learned that her husband was loved by his father, had been sheltered by an adoring mother, served by a huge household, and was destined to be great. Ishmael had been banished, the six sons of Keturah later were sent away with gifts (Gen. 25:5–6), and Abraham could give all he had to Isaac.

Isaac was forty years old when he married Rebekah. And Isaac soon learned, like his father before him, that children are a heritage of the Lord and that he had to live by faith. After twenty years of earnest prayer, faith was rewarded and twin sons were born to Rebekah.

In spite of such a beautiful beginning, it seemed that Isaac and Rebekah began to grow apart. It is a common experience for young couples either to grow closer together as the years go by or to grow apart. Many things can contribute to this oneness or that apartness. With Rebekah and Isaac, the main reason is found in this sentence, "And Isaac loved Esau . . . but Rebekah loved Jacob" (Gen. 25:28).

How adorable and interesting the twins were! Love for these little boys should have brought Isaac and Rebekah closer together; mutually seeking the good of these children should have been their one consuming task. Instead, favoritism pitted one boy against the other and cast the shadows of suspicion, contention, and rivalry into the home.

Another shadow that dimmed the sunshine of happiness was the lack of reverence and respect that Rebekah had for Isaac. Isaac was the least colorful of the three patriarchs. He was a good man but a passive type. He was quiet and retiring and liked to be served.

As a mother's boy, he may have been overly protected, pampered, and pleased, and now Rebekah had to mother him. She was aggressive and gradually assumed more responsibility as Isaac assumed less. At the same time, Rebekah lost admiration and respect for her aging husband, and, considering her treatment of him, it appears that she came to despise him.

The question—*Who is the head of the house?*—has been tossed about for ages, often in jest. This problem has increased as women have become increasingly educated and entered the workplace. Counselors conclude that husbands have a need to be looked up to and appreciated in order to be happy. They insist that every woman *can* and *must* find reasons for admiring and looking up to her husband. Rebekah did not try but went from bad to worse, becoming an eavesdropper, a schemer, and a cheat. Read the story of how she rehearsed with Jacob the great deception she had planned. So the shadows lengthened on the day of one whose morning had begun so fair.

Estrangement

Aging Isaac, his vision so dimmed that even the form of his beloved Esau has become but a moving shadow, is silent and withdrawn as he lies on his couch. The joy of youth, love, and life are gone, except in the measure that it still lives in Esau. Perhaps the strong contrast of his own quiet, more timid outlook has made the rugged, athletic, carefree ways of Esau all the more appealing. Adventurous, openhearted Esau had first place in his father's affections. Even though the heavenly message to Rebekah designated Jacob to be the covenant heir, Isaac quietly determined to give it to Esau.

An event of such importance should have been discussed with Rebekah. Yet how small and mean she appears as she eavesdrops and, with a scheming face, hurriedly calls Jacob. It is an amazing domestic drama that follows. Rebekah plans and executes her scheme to make Jacob the chief inheritor. There was nothing she would not do for Jacob. She loved him more than happiness, than

Isaac, than life itself. Jacob was a man after her own heart. He had a sense of the worth of tomorrow and of spiritual things. He was much like her—ambitious, aggressive, a schemer who knew the thrill of success. Yes, he resembled her family, and all her affections reverted to him.

Though Rebekah's motive may possibly have been good, her method was deplorable. Her deceit cannot be excused, both for what it did to her husband and for what it did to her sons. The favoritism displayed by both parents was sinful. It gave the sons a sense of injustice, of being robbed of the love of a parent. It drove them to the unhappiness of jealousy and rivalry. It led to deceit, which God abhors, to cheating and hate and, finally, to years of separation and fearful distrust of one another.

When Jacob was afraid of being caught, Rebekah replied with determination, "Upon me be thy curse, my son" (Gen. 27:13). What awful words—forever beyond recall! Her consequent penalty of loneliness and heartache were terrible to bear. She had driven her sons apart. Esau must have hated his mother. And Jacob, the accomplice, he hated with the vengeance of murder. After a hurried farewell, Rebekah's beloved Jacob was also lost to her. And the deception she executed so cleverly drove a still wider wedge between herself and her husband.

It was not only Rebekah who suffered but also every member of her family. Her beloved Jacob went out into the world with wrong ideas of right and justice, ignorant of how to get along with others, and with the mistaken notion that sin pays. Christian parents should always try to be honest, fair, and impartial in all their dealings! May they remember that the most powerful lessons are taught by example.

So ends the true story of the romance, failures, and trials of lovely Rebekah, the woman whom Isaac loved.

Suggestions for Discussion

1. List the qualifications Rebekah had as a bride for Isaac. Are they good qualifications for a wife today?

2. What did Isaac have to meditate and pray about?
3. What does the fact that Rebekah comforted Isaac suggest about the duties a wife has to her husband in various circumstances?
4. How should a young man show consideration to parents who give their daughter to him?
5. Favoritism was Rebekah's glaring sin. Discuss the possibility of favoritism in our homes.
6. Social studies reveal that any favoritism shown by parents to their children can cause a serious breakdown in the home structure. Discuss the possible effects it could have.
7. What does the Bible teach us about the respect a wife should have for her husband? See Ephesians 5:22–24, 33.
8. Do you think Rebekah was motivated by her faith in the divine pronouncement that was given to her in Genesis 25:23 when she planned with Jacob to steal the blessing? Or would you say her motive was merely favoritism?
9. What burden did Isaac and Rebekah share? Look up Genesis 26:34–35; 27:46; and 28:1–9. Do parents today have problems like this?
10. What good traits do you find in Rebekah? What bad traits?

Rachel was beautiful and well-favored . . . [but]
Rachel envied her sister.
—Genesis 29:17; 30:1

6

Rachel

Scripture Reading
Genesis 29–35

𝒥or the great majority of us the most absorbing subject in life is love. In a world of sin, hate, and greed, there is no more potent force for good than love. Love for God, love between parents and children, husband and wife, love for home and country, and love for all things beautiful is the antidote against immorality and evil of every kind.

How popular, as well as important, the subject of love is can be proven by a look at the list of books with a love theme and the magazines that regularly carry discussions on such subjects as "All About Love," "How to Keep Your Husband's Affection," and "How Not to Love Your Wife." Special emphasis is placed on the indispensability of love in the home for the preservation of all that is worthwhile in human character and life. The moral breakdown in homes has made us conscious of the need for love, because it is a positive emotion that builds, protects, enriches, and enlarges life.

There is a wide range of meanings for the word *love*. There is

love of money, of power, and of art. There is brotherly love, love of
freedom and country. But a true love between husband and wife is
the most intense love of all. It is the kind of love that goes out of
self to become part of the other. It is love that spontaneously shares
and gives.

One of the most delightful examples in all of history can be found
in the love of Jacob and Rachel.

Rachel Chosen

An interesting part of a love story is invariably the place where
the young couple meet—sometimes in a distant city or away at
college, at a social gathering or, perhaps, at the home of a friend.
The meeting of Rachel and Jacob forms a pastoral scene. Jacob,
alone and on foot, had escaped the anger of his brother. Haunted
by the threats of Esau and the anxiety caused by his mother, he
found no peace until he came to Bethel where Jehovah said, "I am
with thee" (Gen. 28:15). Inspired by new hopes, Jacob hurried east
toward Mesopotamia, the home of his uncle Laban. As he approached Haran, he came to a well in a field with three flocks of
sheep lying by it. He felt at ease with the shepherds and carried on
a friendly conversation with them. Eliezar, Abraham's servant had,
in a previous generation, also halted at a well near here. It was a
well on the edge of the town where women stepped down and low-
ered great pitchers into the water to draw for family use. At such a
well Eliezar met Rebekah.

The well Jacob rested at was in the open fields. It had a large
covering with a hole in the center and was sealed with a heavy
stone that was removed only after all the flocks had come so that
all could share the precious water. Jacob had already learned that
he was near Laban's home, when over the low rolling hills he saw
another flock coming herded by a shepherdess. Imagine his pleasure when he found that the beautiful shepherdess was his cousin
Rachel! He greeted Rachel warmly and kissed her. Then his pent-
up emotions were released, and he wept with joy and thankfulness

to God for bringing him safely to the house of his mother's brother. Rachel, in her excitement, ran all the way home to tell her family that a man who said he was cousin Jacob had come. Jacob was given a hearty welcome by Laban.

It did not take Jacob long to discover that he was in love with beautiful Rachel and that he would do anything to win her. It did not take Laban long, either, to ascertain that Jacob was an ambitious and faithful worker. So, scheming Laban and desperately-in-love Jacob struck a bargain. It was a hard bargain, but because of Jacob's spontaneous love for Rachel the seven years of toil seemed as mere days to him. The happy day came when Jacob had finally earned his bride, but, disappointed and deeply hurt, he learned too late that Laban had cleverly substituted his older daughter, the tender-eyed Leah, for Rachel, with whom he was so much in love. Even after being deceived with Leah, he could not give up Rachel, so he pledged to work another seven years for her.

Rachel was sweet, graceful, and beautiful. Jacob was happy to give fourteen years of his life in long, hard labor for her. People truly in love are always loyal, come what may. To them, sacrifices are nothing—the joy and comfort and love of the other is the acme of desire. We should learn much from the constant devotion of Rachel and Jacob.

Her Character

Although his father Isaac would never have condoned it, Jacob took on, apparently without a qualm, the heathen practice of polygamy and found its inevitably bitter results. Jacob's other wife, Leah, was unattractive but blessed with children. Rachel was beautiful of face and form but did not have children, and this was a catastrophe to her. It made her envious of her sister; it filled her with bitterness and complaints. Instead of angrily blaming Jacob (Gen. 30:1–2), she would have done better by emulating the conduct of her mother-in-law, who made her problems a matter of prayer. Though we can praise her for her desire for children, it was not right for her to rebel against God's providence. Though she so desired motherhood, she could have turned her thoughts outward to others and to loving the children of her sister. In the giving of her maid Bilhah to Jacob, we see also envy, impatience, and an insistence on having her own way (Gen. 30:3–8).

Her Children

Rachel had to learn that children are God's gift, as the mandrake episode clearly indicates (Gen. 30:14–18). (There was a superstition that mandrakes could cure sterility.) To her envious dismay, it was Leah who had another son, although Rachel had made use of the fragrant herbs. When some two years later Joseph was born and her disgrace was removed, she found happiness and peace, for now she saw the Lord's hand on her life. But Rachel, with her strong desire for children, had to feel the full depth of the meaning of the curse pronounced in Paradise, for she died in childbirth when her second son was born. Rachel's whole soul was expressed in her last desperate cry, *Benoni,* "child of grief." The people of Israel could not forget Rachel. The sad cry of that succumbing mother-heart reechoed for centuries until in Bethlehem, near which she died and was buried, there was one day a great weeping and lamentation because of the horrible massacre of many little children (Jer. 31:15; Matt. 2:16–18).

Rachel's untimely death left behind a tiny motherless baby and a grieving husband who, all his life long, had poured out his love upon her. Young Joseph, perhaps a teenager by this time, was left to mourn his mother. Joseph had inherited much of the sweetness and attractiveness of his mother; along with that, God had richly endowed him with great business acumen and nobility of character.

Father Jacob seems to have forgotten the sea of trouble into which his own parents had been cast through favoritism. Although plain coats were fine for the other boys, Joseph had to have one of many colors. He was favored and adored above the other children, which later brought him misery and trouble—but God meant this evil for good. Talented and likable as one of our own children may be, we should be prayerfully vigilant to give all our children the full amount of affection that they need.

Suggestions for Discussion

1. How do you account for Jacob's ease with the shepherds? See Genesis 25:27; 27:9; and 30:29–31.

2. What do you know about the significance of wells in the early days?

3. Do you think it was love at first sight for Rachel and Jacob?

4. The custom of kissing originally had symbolic character. Look up the following references and determine what each denotes: Genesis 27:26; 33:4; 45:15; 48:10; 1 Samuel 10:1; Matthew 26:48; Luke 7:44 – 45; Romans 16:16; and 1 Corinthians 16:20.

5. Do you think the bargain Laban made with Jacob was a fair one? Who made the terms? What custom occasioned it?

6. Explain Rachel's desperation over her barrenness. Is it unusual for a woman to be envious of her sister's children?

7. What does Jacob's reply to Rachel's accusations indicate about each of them?

8. "Love is blind" is a commonplace saying. Are people deeply in love aware of each other's imperfections? Should they be?

9. What can we learn about Rachel from the episode found in Genesis 31, beginning with verse 19?

10. Was the love of Jacob for Rachel constant through the years? See Genesis 33:2.

11. Was Rachel buried with the patriarchs?

12. For what was Rachel remembered?

Happy am I, for the daughters will call me blessed.
—Genesis 30:13

7

Leah

Scripture Reading
Genesis 29:16–35; 30:9–21; 35:23–26

$\mathcal{M}$any beautiful girls from all parts of the United States go to Atlantic City, New Jersey, every year for the annual Miss America contest. Most contestants represent their state; a few are sent by their city or territory. Millions of people watching the telecast program are persuaded that there were never more beautiful girls anywhere.

There was a time when the choice was determined by physical beauty alone. Now, to win the coveted title, talent is just as necessary. To be America's queen of beauty one must be lovely of face and figure and accomplished in some field of art beside.

Centuries ago, in the days of the patriarchs, there were also beautiful girls who were popular, admired, and sought after. We read of beautiful Sarah, the charming Rebekah, lovely Rachel, and many others. Their standards of popularity differed from ours today. Having children was more important than anything else to them. Happy and honored were the girls who had both beauty and a family. Laban and Bethuel blessed beautiful Rebekah and said, "Our sister, be

thou the mother of thousands of millions" (Gen. 24:60). This blessing, indicating the deep desire that lived in the hearts of these Eastern girls, helps us to understand the problems of Leah and her sister
Rachel.

Plain but Tolerated

How intriguing is the story of the substitute bride. What fraud,
suspense, bitterness, and disillusionment is shown in this moving
episode. Not even the greatest playwright has equaled such drama!
What the life story of Leah lacks in beauty it more than makes up
in interest. Some say that the lives of Rachel and Leah are so closely
knit that they cannot be studied apart, but we will take Leah out of
the shadow of the "beautiful and well-favored" Rachel and find
that she is worth knowing.

Jacob loved Rachel so much that he had eyes for no one else. His
thoughts were filled with her charm, and her smile only made his
love the more ardent and passionate. Just the sight of her at the end
of the day, or after a few weeks of being away with the flocks, made
him forget his weariness in a moment. For the plain and unassum-
ing sister Leah, he had only a cousinly remark or two!

All her life Leah had seen admiring glances turned her sister's
way. As she grew to womanhood, she became acutely conscious of
her own plain face and figure in comparison with her younger
sister's, and of her dull eyes that, even when she laughed, did not
sparkle. When she saw that her beautiful sister had completely cap-
tured the heart of the handsome young man from the hill country
of Canaan, her longing for love and romance became all the more
intense. Hidden deep in her heart, a love grew for Jacob. She would
have given much to be loved as Rachel was.

Considering how all-important marriage was to girls of her day,
it must have distressed Leah, who was the eldest, to be passed by.
And so it is understandable that, when father Laban came to her
with his plan to deceive Jacob, she willingly entered into the scheme.
Whether it was right to deceive her sister seems to have been of

minor importance. To carry out this deception was comparatively easy, for in these days the bride was quietly, and in darkness, ushered into the tent of the groom.

The "mother-in-law problem" shifts ground here, for beginning on his wedding night it was from his father-in-law that Jacob had constant friction and interference. How could anyone respect a father who breaks a solemn promise, deeply wrongs his young daughter, defrauds his nephew, and practically prostitutes his other daughter? How could his family, plunged into distress and consequent family problems, expect sincere devotion and wise counsel from him in the future? How the lame excuse of Laban must have shocked and hurt Jacob! For the first time, sly Jacob, who had deceived his own father and cheated his brother, felt poignantly the pain of being deceived himself. And so it is with us. We do not see the harm in a bit of cheating, lying, or gossiping until we are cheated against, lied to, and gossiped about ourselves. Until we ourselves are injured, we do not see how mean and evil it is to injure someone else.

Comparatively few of us are really beautiful. Most of us are just plain Leahs. It is not wrong to admire beauty, nor is it wrong to be concerned about our appearance. Charm, poise, and good taste in dress and manners can be acquired by all, and an ordinary woman with a charming, well-rounded personality can be more attractive than a petulant, self-willed beauty. We find in Leah—unloved, unsought, undesired, and plain—the qualities of a spiritually sensitive woman. Woman's greatest attractiveness is still found in a meek and quiet spirit, with the adornment of love for God and man combining to make a personality magnetic in its warmth and loveliness.

Unloved but Honored

The problems that constantly arose in this polygamous home, in which two sisters vied for the love of the same man, were many—surely many more than history records. Leah gave to Jacob his first four sons, and Rachel, racked with jealousy, had to listen every day to the cooing and laughter of her sister's children. Though Rachel had Jacob's love, his love for his sons compelled her to draw him toward her all the more selfishly. Leah loved Jacob too, but her love was not reciprocated. Watching Jacob's undying passion for her sister must have made her miserable with longing. Leah wanted, with all her heart, what every woman wants from the man she loves—a constancy in love that is deep, protective, and considerate. It is deeply inherent in the nature of woman to thrive in a truly loving relationship. It was for the love of Jacob that Leah and her sister wrestled in spirit and mind throughout their lives. Only once do we read that they were united in mind and purpose, and that was in their attitude toward their father (Gen. 31).

We can ascertain how much Leah missed the love of her husband in the account of the birth of her sons (Gen. 29:31–35; 30:17–20). Repeatedly, we see that she hoped her children would eventually unite Jacob's heart with her own. She was as much Jacob's wife as Rachel was, and he owed her a full share of his affection. How hard it must have been for the tender and loving Leah to have her husband withdraw his love from her. There was a day when Leah imitated her favored rival's bad feelings and gave her maid Zilpah to Jacob. We are disappointed, too, when we see her quarreling and bartering with Rachel for Jacob's attentions (Gen. 30:15). As the children grew older, her cares increased, for we see the sad results of favoritism in the jealousy among the eleven brothers.

Rachel's despair over her childlessness drove her to bitter jealousy and angry accusations. Envied and neglected, Leah seems to have acquired a quiet and mild disposition, and her marital problems drove her to find help and solace from the Lord. She possessed the faith that prays and trusts and praises God for all things. This we can know from the names she gives to her sons. She must finally and fully have entered into Jacob's life after the untimely death of beloved Rachel. We conclude that she died in Canaan, for she did not go along with Jacob to Egypt. She was buried beside Sarah and Abraham, Isaac and Rebekah in the cave of Macpelah, where Jacob later was laid to rest with her.

Though Jacob had not chosen Leah, God had favored and chosen her to be the ancestress of the Savior. In the book of Ruth, she is honored because she "did build the house of Israel" (Ruth 4:11) for she was the mother of eight of its tribes.

Suggestions for Discussion

1. Think of at least two motives Laban may have had for deceiving Jacob with Leah.
2. Leah's name means "dull," "weary," "yearning." Show how the meaning of her name was portrayed in her life.
3. If we are plain Leahs, should we consider it a cause for complaint? How much may a Christian woman do about her appearance? Can she do anything about her personality? If so, what?
4. What does Leviticus 18:18 say about marrying sisters?
5. Did Jacob really hate Leah? See Genesis 29:30–31.
6. How important is love in marriage? Do you approve of marriage for companionship or for financial security?
7. Name Leah's sons. What do their names mean?
8. Leah wanted nothing more than to have a family. Does our high standard of living and the modern economic status of women devalue family life?

She . . . went out to see the daughters of the land.
—Genesis 34:1

8

𝒟*inah*

Scripture Reading
Genesis 34

𝒯his story of a young girl's indiscretion and consequent dishonor is not pleasant to relate. It involves a subject not easy to discuss and commonly hushed among us. It is pleasant and inspiring to read of the courage and achievements of a lovely lady, but the story we read in Genesis 34 is one of moral laxity and barbaric revenge.

We are told much about Dinah's brothers—the strengths and weaknesses of their characters, the importance of their positions and influence in the history of the old world, and of their places in the history of redemption. Though we learn nothing of the life of Dinah beyond this miserable tale, without a doubt this event had its place in the development of the kingdom and is of value for our times.

As twentieth century mothers, we are constantly made aware of the laxity of morals. Reluctance to speak of closely personal matters with our daughters may contribute to an ignorance of the true facts of life and a consequent misunderstanding and lack of harmony in the family relationships our children establish. It might be well to face the truth—we cannot always avoid the unpleasant and difficult tasks attached to Christian motherhood.

Precious Little Dinah

For such a little girl, Dinah, the darling daughter of Jacob, had seen much excitement since the day she was hoisted high on a camel with her mother Leah and spirited away from the home of her grandfather in Padanaram. She knew something was afoot, young as she was, when her father called her mother and aunt Rachel to the fields for a secret meeting. As any little five-year-old would, she perhaps tried to help with the frenzied packing. After several days of riding as fast as possible with such an unwieldy procession and of eating around new fires every night, there was sudden consternation in the camp. She saw, from afar, grandfather and his servants raising an angry cloud of dust as they pushed their huge beasts to a fast gallop. The darkly ferocious face of Laban must have filled her with fear as she clutched the wide skirts of her trembling mother.

More awful was the agitation of the family when news came that fierce uncle Esau was coming to meet them with his formidable four hundred men. She always remembered how the children had clung close to their mothers through the night while father prayed and wrestled with an angel across the brook. She wondered about the angels who visited her father and left him with such peace and strength and hope. She was as pleased as the rest when each successive problem was amicably settled, and she was taught to pray and give God praise for every blessing.

Happy and carefree were the years she lived at Succoth in the valley of the Jordan, east of the river. There, Jacob had built a house and booths for the cattle. After a number of years, Jacob moved with his cumbersome caravan of flocks and family across the Jordan westward and camped in the Shechem valley between Mount Ebal and Mount Gerizim. Jacob bought land from Hamor, the Hittite prince, so the property on which they lived was their own. How meaningful to the large family was the event of the raising of the altar at this place to the God of the covenant, on whom every blessing depended.

An Adventurous Teenager

For Dinah, who was by this time perhaps fifteen years old, there were other things to do and see. The strange city of Shalem nearby offered greater fascination for Dinah than did her Father's nomadic settlement or even the sacred altar about which the family knelt to do homage. Dinah was young, and the different and unknown attracted her—she was *grown up* now. She had outgrown running about in the sun and picking wild flowers. There were other exotic flowers of pleasure to be picked from life, and she meant to find them!

Dinah had every blessing: a spiritually sensitive mother, a devout and wealthy father, and eleven brothers who adored their only sister. She was taught that those in the covenant had a special charge to live a perfect life—holy and separate from the world. Because she was an only daughter, she was likely adored and pampered and allowed to have her own way. We suspect that she was a pretty girl, resembling her Aunt Rachel more than her plain mother. We can suppose that her mother dressed her in the most becoming gowns and veils she could procure and that she felt sorry for lovely Dinah among so many rough, bronzed brothers. Though her mother may have known that she pined for the friendship of the Hittite girls, it was hard to deny pert Dinah any pleasure.

One of the many heathen festivals was in progress when Dinah arranged her hair and veil with special care and left her mother's tent to see the world, its styles and pleasures, by herself. With eyes big with curiosity and innocence, Dinah happily joined the bevy of city girls. Life in the city seemed convivial and so different from the quiet of the valley.

When Shechem, the son of Prince Hamor, saw the attractive and vivacious Dinah, he fell in love with her and desired her so much that "he took her, and lay with her, and defiled her" (Gen. 34:2). For the young and venturesome Dinah, her pleasurable contact with the world had an abrupt and involved climax. She was held captive by the young Hittite's charm and declarations of love.

A Distressed Family

While Dinah was still being detained in Shechem's house, Jacob heard what Hamor's son had done. Father Jacob was shocked into silence, sorrow, and, perhaps, indecision as to how he should cope with the situation. The brothers would want to be consulted in this serious matter concerning their sister, so Jacob waited. In the meantime, Shechem's father came to offer a large dowry and the hand of his son in honorable marriage.

To the sons, who were called in from the field, the act of Shechem was an unspeakable outrage. Debasing the daughter of the head of the theocratic line, who was therefore under special obligations to live a holy life, was shamefully wicked. Their anger reached unreasonable proportions, and their retaliation was horrible. They plotted against and deceived the Shechemites, abused their sacred sacrament, then massacred and pillaged the entire city of Shalem. Anger is a human emotion, but it must be controlled so it does not become a destructive force. The horrible crime the brothers perpetrated was far greater than the sin of Shechem, who would never have met Dinah if she had not been enticed by worldly pleasures to begin with.

We can hardly understand the mild reproof Jacob gave his sons, for he felt keenly the sin and horror of their dastardly revenge (Gen. 49:5–7). Perhaps he had indulged them in their youth and now was afraid to reprove them. Perhaps this is why we, too, are often afraid to reprove our grown children. "Parents, you are the law in the child's life," say psychologists today. "Children obey your parents," says God's Word. Why do we let our little children disobey us constantly? "Perhaps we are trying to spare our own feelings," said a radio counselor who went on to say, "We hate the unpleasantness of a tussle with them. But cry-babies (which they become when they know they can get their own way), young or old, never get along in this world. Parents who correct and insist on obedience make their children strong."

What catastrophic results this one seemingly innocent act of Dinah had! She lost her fair fame, brought trouble to her father's house, dishonored his good name and involved her brothers, who brought untold misery to an entire city. Though teenagers think they are "wise" and like to be independent, they still are immature in their thinking. It is no accident that the Creator placed children in the care of parents for so many years, for youth need the loving counsel of those who have learned by living. The story of Dinah lays a tremendous challenge at the door of every mother to show her children what things are of true worth and of abiding value.

Suggestions for Discussion

1. Dinah left her quiet environment for excitement in the city. Is the old question "What is there for our young people to do?" a valid one? Should the church provide recreation and entertainment for them?
2. Our children have the same challenge Dinah had—they must learn to live independently and wisely. How conscious of this are we? Our children?
3. Should we have more sermons devoted to young people and their problems?
4. What kind of a young man was Shechem? What moral obligations did he have to his father's house? Did he try to make amends for forcing Dinah, or were his efforts selfish?
5. A youth counselor said, "Know where your children are and with whom they go about." Is that a solution to delinquency? Discuss how this could be worked out.
6. Why do you suppose there are so many accounts of sexual immorality in the Bible? Do you think there is greater tendency toward this kind of sin than to other kinds?

7. Is anger a legitimate emotion? Should anger be repressed? If so, to what extent?

8. Read about the revenge meted out by the brothers. How were Jacob and his family affected by it?

9. Was the accusation of Dinah's brothers in verse 31 justified?

10. It is easy to find the moral for youth in Dinah's story. What can mothers learn from it?

And the woman took the child, and nursed it. And the child grew. . . .
—Exodus 2:9–10

9

Jochebed

Scripture Reading
Exodus 1; 2:1–11; 6:20; Numbers 26:59;
Hebrews 11:23–27

A sweet young mother said with deep concern: "I want to read all I can and know as much as possible, so I can help my little children grow up right." There are many such mothers, for which we thank God and take courage for tomorrow. Every faithful mother is stirred with a keen sense of her responsible role as she looks into the trusting and questioning eyes of her little ones. The degree of interest little children have in everything in their small sphere is unpredictable. It is a new wonder-world, and they must touch, taste, and try everything within reach. Mother is always at the center of the little child's universe, and busy little minds soon find that even mothers can be "tried."

During the last two decades there has been so much specialization in the field of child training that mothers have often been made to feel completely inadequate. The fearful word *discipline* was shelved for the sake of the child's budding personality. But mother found that leaving dishes to pile up in the kitchen sink to devote all her time to every desire and whim of her child (though many demands were good in themselves) benefited no one. It only served to make that child into a tiny dictator. Frustrated, parents turned again to psychologists and books on child training.

Finally, the realization began to dawn that the Creator, in designing the human parent, was also quite an expert, and parents now are advised to call on their own resources, abilities, and common sense, the controlling factor being loving interest in the welfare of the child. Discipline is no longer a weapon handed down from the dark ages. Now we are advised that *discipline* has the same root as *disciple* and that, through creative leadership, parents must make disciples of their children. Children must no longer hold the reins. They must be given values, ideals, and moral principles to live by. We, as Christians, must add to the advice of the experts in saying that we must teach the fear of God, which is the beginning of wisdom and the basis for a well-adjusted life.

There is no greater charge in all the world than that of parenthood. Though atomic energy may blow the world to bits, the souls of men live on. Though you become old and the things that once meant so much to you are forgotten, the character you have been instrumental in building lives on indelibly to impress others. Turn to good source books on child guidance if you will, in your attempt to do a good job, but do not neglect the Lord's advice in His Word and to ask for wisdom in your prayers. You are His vicegerent, and what He tells you to do will not swing like a pendulum on a clock from decade to decade—for His truth is the same yesterday, today, and forever.

Jochebed's Faith

This story, which starts simply, tells us that the great thing is not so much *who you are* as *what you do* with your life. How you meet life's challenges and responsibilities—that is what counts. We do not even find Jochebed's name in this brief but moving account of the birth of her third child, Moses. And how unpretentiously it begins: "And there went a man of the house of Levi, and took to wife a daughter of Levi. And the woman conceived, and bare a son" (Exod. 2:1–2). But the exciting story that follows has all the elements of a fairy tale, with its pathos, suspense, and happy ending.

Jochebed belonged to a race once favored but now afflicted. About four hundred years before, Joseph had become the great benefactor of his people. The family of seventy souls, besides the wives of the sons of Jacob, had migrated from Canaan to Egypt to escape death by famine. A kind Pharaoh had given Jacob's family the land of Goshen where a new era began for them. The Israelites had to change from a nomadic life to farming and to life in the cities, and the Lord blessed them abundantly. They had grown great in might and had multiplied exceedingly until, at the time of the exodus, they numbered hundreds of thousands and had great wealth in the form of flocks and possessions. A new Pharaoh, who knew little of the famed benefactor of Egypt and cared less, feared this strong people who were now almost a nation within a nation. This king determined to curb the people of Israel by making them slave laborers, but the more he oppressed them the stronger they grew until, in final desperation, he issued a child-murder edict to the midwives (Exod. 1). These women feared God and disobeyed the king, for which God dealt well with them. But Pharaoh was determined, and the days were indeed dark for the suffering slaves when the king charged all his people to destroy every son born to the Hebrews.

In these days, when the people groaned under fierce lashes and pressing burdens, when fear mingled with the agony of every travailing mother, Jochebed gave birth to her third child. Seeing her robust, beautiful baby, she covered him close to her side. Her heart cried out to God with intense longing. Some say that she saw in her baby a child of destiny. It is agreed by all that he was an exceptionally fine and beautiful child. One thing she *knew:* the baby was God's gift, and such gifts are not given to be destroyed but to be loved and nurtured and then given back to Him as precious jewels to make bright His crown. She also knew that disobedience to the king's command, if detected, would mean severe punishment and certain death for the child.

In all Jochebed did, her faith was pivotal. It is only because of her faith that we know her at all. All her actions hinged on her faith in the love, power, and providence of God. The voice of the same Spirit who enabled her guides us in our perplexities and problems: "When thou passest through the waters, I will be with thee; and through the rivers, they shall not overflow thee: when thou walkest through the fire, thou shalt not be burned; neither shall the flame kindle upon thee. For I am the LORD thy God, the Holy One of Israel, thy Saviour" (Isa. 43:2–3). "Why are ye fearful, O ye of little faith?" Jesus said in Matthew 8:26. Your faith and hope must be in God, Peter tells us in 1 Peter 1:21. "And this is the victory that overcometh the world, even our faith" (1 John 5:4). Faith is seen by its works, and Jochebed could say, "The Lord is my helper, and I will not fear what man shall do unto me" (Heb. 13:6). Perfect faith casts out fear, and so it is that among the heroes of faith in Hebrews 11:23 we find the parents of Moses. "By faith Moses, when he was born, was hid three months of his parents, because they saw he was a proper child; and they were not afraid of the king's commandment." What a wearing vigil Jochebed kept for three months, as she hid the baby from the prying eyes and ears of neighbors. How she must have constantly called to her only Protector with prayer that laid hold, with both hands and all her heart, on God's promises. It was Jochebed's firm faith that gave her the strength for the task.

We see that her faith was strong. She showed ingenuity as she wove a tiny ark from the long, pliant stems of the papyrus plant, which, it was said, was a protection against crocodiles. What a positive faith she had that God would protect her child as she worked to make the ark comfortable and watertight.

Her faith was not without wisdom when she placed the child in the bulrushes at the river's edge. It was there that Pharaoh's daughter went to bathe each day and she was, perhaps, the only one with the power to save the child, should God so incline her heart. Then Miriam was set to watch, and Jochebed prayed, we are sure, as only a woman who knew both her need and what her God could do.

Jochebed's faith was remarkably rewarded. God inclined the heart of the heathen princess to be pitiful and to save the goodly child. What a release from the months of tension! And what pure joy sang in the heart of this courageous mother when she was called to nurse her own son! No one in the tiny group clustered on the river bank could know how stupendous the implications of the Princess's decision were when she said to Jochebed, "Take this child away, and nurse it for me, and I will give thee thy wages" (Exod. 2:9). We see that when God wanted to raise up a great leader He placed him in a home with godly parents to teach, train, and make strong the child who would one day need positive convictions and courage for leadership.

Jochebed was given a sacred trust. She knew that it was not the princess but God who was her real employer, and what a burden was laid on her heart to plant faith and love for the covenant God in the heart of her little boy. She knew his education would be extensive but pagan when, as a young prince, he would be taught all the learning of ancient Egypt.

It is noteworthy that this precious child, through whom infinite blessings would come to the world, was not left in the care of a heathen for his early training but to a godly mother. Jochebed was a good mother, for she was willing and eager for her task. Many mothers are not so happy about being tied down to the constant care and responsibilities of child rearing. Many feel burdened and distraught and complain because they do not have time for other pleasurable pursuits. Jochebed was called, not to make the social register nor even to such noble things as lecturing for the freedom of a slave people, but to "take this child and nurse him." Hers was the privilege of loving and giving, and of making her child strong for life in all of its ruggedness. That is still the first duty of mothers.

Her Fame

Jochebed is nowhere vividly described, as many Old Testament women are. The record of Jochebed's life concerns only the first few years of the life of Moses, yet her greatness is monumental. Her name is imperishable, for her fame lives on in the lives of her re-markable children. To them she transmitted character and the challenge of a "living-faith-for-life" view. She becomes an example to us, not because of any great thing she did but in how wisely and well she served as a mother.

Here we have a mother who gave her oldest son to the priesthood and her youngest son to be a great prophet and civic leader. She brought up her daughter to take a prominent place of service among her people. Without a doubt, the major influence in the lives of each can be attributed to the conscientious training given by a devoted mother.

Her son Moses was the foremost man of his age. More than that, save Jesus, Moses is the greatest man that ever set foot in this world. He conversed with God in His very presence and with Jesus at the Transfiguration. The book he wrote did more than any other book did to banish the world's wrongs, and people still live by its principles today. He was the great emancipator of his people, a type of Christ, the Savior of the world.

Moses was a man of sterling character. He believed that the future belonged not to sin but to God. He was a man of decision. By faith, he looked away from worldly pleasures and the splendor of his position in the court of Egypt. He could say no to sin and yes to God, for he chose reproach as did Christ. By faith, he was unafraid of hardship and so was able to render great service to his people and to the whole world. Though he was undoubtedly influenced by the high standard of morality present among the Egyptians of his day, it was faith in his mother's God that made him great.

Jochebed's background speaks of holiness, for she and Amram belonged to the tribe of Levi, and she passed down this heritage to Aaron who was about three years older than Moses. He became the first high priest of Israel and was set apart, with his entire family, for the priesthood. He was charged by God with various privileges, duties, and regulations for the Lord's services. He was an excellent speaker and was directed by God to assist Moses.

Mother Jochebed taught her daughter Miriam to trust God and

fearlessly take every opportunity to serve Him. Miriam is the first woman we read about who is interested in her people as a nation and, assisting her brothers Aaron and Moses, she rendered a great service to Israel (Mic. 6:4).

So Jochebed's children were what good Christians want their children to be, people who enter into every possible sphere and situation with the single purpose of bringing glory to God. She gave to each of her children the training and sensitivity of purpose that made them choose for right, for truth, and for God. She is a good example to modern mothers who allow their children to be influenced for hours at a time by questionable television programs or are relieved to pack off noisy little ones to nursery school. She lights the way for those of us who perhaps too often leave our sensitive little children to baby-sitters for hours. What kind of a man would Moses have been if his training and inspiration had come from such sources? What of his character, sense of justice, scale of values?

Jochebed hitched her wagon and her children's wagon to the highest star—that of special service to the Lord. Today the field is white to the harvest—but where are the laborers (Matt. 9:35–38)?

Suggestions for Discussion

1. We read in Exodus 2 that the mother of Moses was the daughter of Levi. Where do we find her name?
2. Did the parents see anything extraordinary about their baby? See Exodus 2:2; Acts 7:20; and Hebrews 11:23.
3. How do you account for the kindness of the princess?
4. Was Jochebed's faith reasonable? Prove by other examples the power of God to preserve life in the midst of trial.
5. Whose work is it to train the child—the parents, the church, or the school?
6. What are the most impressionable years of life?
7. Make an honest evaluation of the present and possible future effects that our television programs might have on

our children. How will what they see on television affect their conception of God's providence, love, and truth? How will it affect their love for other people and their sense of right and wrong?

8. Suggestion: Read a good article or a good book on child training and evaluate it.

9. Talk about the ideals that parents should have in working with their little ones.

10. How many things can you find good and exemplary in Jochebed?

For I brought thee up out of the land of Egypt, . . .
and I sent before thee Moses, Aaron, and Miriam.
—Micah 6:4

10

Miriam

Scripture Reading
Exodus 2:1–10; 15:20–21;
Numbers 12; 20:1; 26:59

The book of Exodus is an extremely interesting book. It is the record of the interval of 360 years between the death of Joseph and the giving of the law on Mount Sinai. In the opening chapter, we find that the people whom God had foreseen when He had called Abraham alone (Isa. 51:2) had become a numerous and strong people. Exodus deals mainly with the departure of the Israelites from Egypt and is the story, with many sidelights, of their march to Canaan, the promised land of Genesis 12:1.

Besides being interesting historically, Exodus tells us something of ancient geography and art, and of how the knowledge of ethics and jurisprudence was established through the medium of Moses. The law is given to the people and the theocracy formed; detailed plans are given for the tabernacle, and the priesthood is established. Every event recorded is epoch making in the development of Israel as a nation. Three people figure prominently in this development:

Moses, Aaron, and Miriam. Preeminent, above all, is Jehovah, the head of His chosen people.

Nowhere in Scripture is the reality of the living God more plainly seen than in this book. Those who think God is in His distant heaven, far removed from the doings of humankind, have only to read Exodus to find that He is an infinitely great being to whom all are subject. His omnipotence as seen in His mighty acts (Exod. 14:13, 26–31), His constant protection of His people (Exod. 13:21–22), His anger with sin (Exod. 32:33), and His saving grace (Exod. 32:14) stand out in bold relief. In 33:17–23, continuing through 34:10, there is a majestic picture of the Supreme Being, Lord of all. May we, like Moses, make haste to bow our heads to the earth and worship.

A Precocious Child

Miriam is the first woman mentioned in the Bible whose interest was national and whose mission was patriotic. For many years, Miriam held a unique place among her people. In Micah 6:4 we read, "For I brought thee up out of the land of Egypt, and redeemed thee out of the house of servants; and I sent before thee Moses, Aaron, and Miriam."

First, we are permitted a glimpse into her childhood. Miriam was the sister of Aaron and Moses, and the daughter of Jochebed and Amram. She lived in Egypt, perhaps in the Nile River valley near the city of On. This was the seat of the ancient kings and is now the area of Cairo.

The Pharaoh who ruled was heartless and cruel. He feared the increasing power of the Israelites and worried over the possibilities of their becoming a fifth column that might turn on the Egyptians if they were attacked by enemies from without. He heaped extreme hardships on the people, hoping to break their spirits. To decrease their numbers and strength he next decreed that all male babies must die. The horror of this edict struck home to the heart of Miriam when her new baby brother was born. Miriam, who was about thirteen years old at this time, understood that this created an emergency.

The secret scheme to try to save the new baby, plotted behind the closed doors of the small slave hut, made no impression on Aaron, who was a toddler of three. But it stirred Miriam deeply, for in every little girl there is a mother's heart.

It might well be that Miriam picked the stems of the papyrus for her mother and stood by hushing the baby as her mother wove the ark. It was likely under the cover of darkness that she helped her mother launch the basket with its precious cargo. Her mother knew she was brave and dependable when she set her to watch what would become of the baby. Imagine Miriam's anxiety when the first streaks of dawn brought lowing herds to the river and the sounds of a world awakening. Fear and faith struggle when she hears voices, and she sees that it is Pharaoh's daughter, Themutis, and her maidens who have come to bathe. Breathlessly she watches, eyes intent on the face of the princess, observing her every reaction as the tiny ark is lifted onto the sand and opened. She shows poise and finesse as she chooses the opportune moment to approach the honorable princess. Miriam must avoid any risk of identity and, discreetly, she says neither too much nor too little.

From this event we conclude that Miriam was a precocious girl, displaying much more intelligence and wisdom than the average child of thirteen. We also know that her mother brought her up well, for she was taught at an early age to assist her mother, to care for her brothers, and to assume responsibility. In a recent issue of the *Readers Digest* there was an article by a judge who said, "Let's allow our teenagers to work." Perhaps he is on the right track. Apparently, both Miriam's inherent character traits and her early training worked together to make her a great woman.

A Patriotic Old Maid

Twice forty years have passed before we meet Miriam again in the pages of the Bible. During this time she doubtless lived with her parents, enduring all kinds of hardships. She had grown up in the depressing atmosphere of fear, of unalleviated suffering, with the talk of brick-making, the progress of the store cities, and of vicious taskmasters. Yet, through all these years her spirit was not broken. As a prophetess, she must have gone about doing good, keeping alive in her people a faith in God and a hope for a better day. She is the first woman the Bible honors with the title of prophetess (Exod. 15:20).

It appears that she never married; why, we are not told. Miriam was a brilliant woman, far more intelligent and thoughtful than most women of her time, and perhaps she was so involved in her career that she had no other real interests. The particular career to which Miriam felt called was that of assisting her brothers in the building of a new nation.

One author calls her the grand patriotic old maid. He goes on to say that it is not necessary for a woman to get married to be useful, for records show that some of the finest women who ever lived were unmarried. He detests flings made at them and says that most of these women do not marry because they choose to stay single. They are intelligent women who follow a career or, in other ways, find a useful place in society. Many render exemplary service as Sunday school teachers, in works of charity, and some in the service of music as Miriam also did. No matter what may be said about the place of women in the progress of the church, Miriam's position teaches us that the Lord does use women in building His kingdom.

As the second scene in her life opens, we see her as a prominent national figure. Her brother Moses has returned as the great emancipator (after a forty-year exile), and Aaron has become a prominent character among his people. Wondrous miracles attesting to the God-given mission of her illustrious brothers have taken place. Israel's deliverance has been accomplished and the people are free and safe while the Red Sea rolled relentlessly over the army of the Egyptians, those who for scores of years had held them in painful bondage.

The ecstatic feelings of joy and gratitude for such a marvelous deliverance flooded the heart of Moses and were expressed in a most beautiful song of victory and thanksgiving to Jehovah (Exod. 15:1–19). This is called the song of Moses and Miriam and is the first, and one of the loveliest, of the Hebrew poems on record. Miriam's work seems to have been with the women, and we see her in the hour of triumph helping them as the Israelites are being separated, by Egyptian custom, into distinct groups of men and women. While Moses directed some six hundred thousand men, she conducted an equal number of women in this joyous song of victory. We can almost see Miriam—courageous, commanding, and radiant—striking her tambourine as she directs the women who dance and play their instruments. Again and again she and the women come in with the grand chorus, while Moses leads the huge company of men in singing the verses. Over, before, and behind them was the beneficent presence of God, and in their hearts was exultation, fresh courage, and new hope. What a glorious view of Miriam at the head of Israel's women, almost an equal with her brother.

A Petty Woman

We leave Miriam in her hour of triumph and turn the pages to Numbers 12. What a contrast we see! She has had a spiritual fall, and there is a tragic blot on her career. It was caused by something we would least expect. She has spoken against her brother Moses! The limitations in Miriam's character are brought to light, and we see that her heart lacked genuine humility and contentment. She knew that she was able and was proud of it, and she was ambitious for greater political powers.

She saw that Moses was more prominent than she and became jealous of him. Envious, bitter thoughts must have been brewing in her heart for a long time before they came out in hurtful propaganda against Moses, who had married a Cushite. Being a prophetess, she may have had strong and justified feelings against marrying outside of the nation. She made a mistake, however, when she made her complaint public, imperiling the authority of Moses.

That her criticism of Moses was only a pretext for her real feeling is indicated when we hear her angry retort that Moses has no monopoly on divine communication, and that she and Aaron are leaders, in every sense, as much as he. The Lord heard her and called a meeting of all three parties. God looked into her heart and perceived that the real cause for her agitation was not the Cushite, but envy of Moses.

The Almighty is angry (Num. 12:4–9). How does she dare attack the man who has done so well the great work committed to his trust! The great Defender of Moses makes it plain to Miriam that her claim is not true. He appears to prophets in visions and dreams, but He has elected to speak by mouth and in visible form to Moses, so setting Moses apart and above other prophets. God has made Miriam a prophetess and Aaron a priest, but the work of Moses extends to every department in all God's house.

Miriam's responsibility was to do well the task that was hers. Could it be that we are ever guilty of the sin of Miriam? Have we ever exposed the shortcomings or told mean little things about someone of whom we are jealous? No quality distorts the heart and mind more than envy, and Miriam should have been happy about her brother's good favor. She could have done an immeasurable amount of good by giving Moses her wholehearted support in his almost superhuman task. It is good to know that God gives to each his own task, and that task must be done humbly, gratefully, and to the best of our ability.

> My Father has need of the birds and the flowers,
> And a place for each beautiful tree
> And so I am sure in His Wonderful plan
> There's a place and a mission for me.
>
> So wherever I go, and all that I do,
> I crave a clear vision to see
> My place in my Father's own wonderful plan
> My task and His blessing for me.
> —Author Unknown

God Himself exposed Miriam's sin and rebuked her. He further put His mark of displeasure on her, for in a moment she was covered with horrible leprosy in its last stages and, ill and shamed, she was shut out of the camp. She who coveted honor was now in dishonor. It was in answer to the prayer of the one she had wronged that she was restored to health and to fellowship with her people, but her deep desire to enter the promised land was not fulfilled. She died and was buried in the wilderness the year before Israel entered Canaan.

By God's grace Miriam will sing again with the host of the redeemed, for all did drink of the same spiritual drink. They drank of the spiritual rock that followed them, and that rock was Christ. "Stand[ing] on the sea of glass, having the harps of God. They sing the song of Moses the servant of God, and the song of the Lamb, saying, Great and marvelous are thy works, Lord God Almighty" (Rev. 15:2–3).

Suggestions for Discussion

1. What does the name *Miriam* mean?
2. What character traits do we see in Miriam as a child?
3. Is it good for young children to carry responsibility? What kind? How much?
4. How can we be our brother's keeper in the family circle? In the community of believers?
5. What was Miriam's contribution to the building of the new nation?
6. What roles do women play in the building of the kingdom today? What do you think of political involvement?
7. Was Miriam's claim in Numbers 12:2 true or false? Explain your answer.
8. What was her sin? Is this kind of sin prevalent now? What are its effects on those who commit it? On others involved?
9. What qualities of heart and mind must we have in order to perform our tasks to the glory of God?

By faith the harlot Rahab perished not with them that believed not.
—Hebrews 11:31

11

Rahab

Scripture Reading
Joshua 2; 6:17–25; Hebrews 11:31;
James 2:25

Forty years had passed since that dark midnight when there was a great cry in all Egypt for their firstborn dead. That same day a slave people had marched boldly toward the Red Sea and freedom, led by Moses, Miriam, and Aaron. These many years, they had pitched camp in the desert many times over. Now, in the last year of sojourn, all three of these remarkable leaders had died. Moses, though one hundred twenty years old, was still strong and vigorous when, after a long look at the land of Canaan, he died on Mount Nebo. Before his death, he had publicly conferred the task of leadership on his prime minister, Joshua, who was a godly man and full of the spirit of wisdom. Moses had also pointed out the bounds of Israel's inheritance and given specific directions for its division (Num. 34).

The land west of the Jordan was already occupied by Gad, Reuben, and the half-tribe of Manasseh. They were busy building homes for

their families and folds for their animals by the time Joshua replaced Moses. Across the Jordan to the west lay the land for the rest
of the tribes. As Joshua thought of the gigantic task before him, he
heard the voice of Jehovah, "As I was with Moses, so I will be with
thee: I will not fail thee, nor forsake thee. Be strong and of a good
courage: for unto this people shalt thou divide for an inheritance
the land, which I sware unto their fathers to give them. . . . Thou
shalt have good success" (Josh. 1:5–6, 8).

The Outsider

The people who inhabited the land west of the Jordan were the
powerful Canaanites. It appears that they were divided into petty
kingdoms, each having its own king who, when occasion demanded,
could form powerful alliances (Josh. 9:1–2). They were protected
by mountains, the strong flowing Jordan, and the Mediterranean
Sea. Their cities were well fortified. They were a cultured people.
Their commercial achievements were well known, and they carried on peaceful trade with other countries. The Canaanites were
an idolatrous people whose worship was sensuous and atrociously
cruel. Their fertility rites and human sacrifices to Baal were shocking to the Israelites, whose rules of life were based on the Law of
Moses. The Canaanites' cup of iniquity was full. It was among these
people that Rahab lived. She was one of them. Perhaps it was in the
service of Ashteroth that she became a harlot and, as such, she
could even have attained respect in the eyes of the Canaanites.

Rahab lived in Jericho, the strongest of the fortified cities of
Canaan. This ancient "City of Palms," as it was known, was surrounded and protected by two walls about fifteen feet apart. The
walls, though not high, were wide and sturdy, and houses made of
sun dried bricks, supported by timbers, were built over the gap.
Rahab's house occupied a place on the wall.

Jericho, with its bleached flat rooftops, was situated in a green
valley, picturesque with palm trees. The well-watered area of the Jordan was lush and fertile, and the warm climate of the plain was well

suited to the raising of luscious fruits and abundant crops. It was a land flowing with milk and honey, and the people were prosperous.

This was the land that Joshua was to claim for Israel. He had God's sacred promise of victory but, as a military leader, he had to plan wisely. He chose Jericho as the starting point of his campaign. His strategy may have involved separating the kings of the North from the kings of the South. From the pleasant acacia groves, east of the Jordan and directly west of Jericho, Joshua sent two young men as spies to the "City of Fragrance." The Jordan was swift and turbulent as it dropped rapidly to below sea level in this area, and the adventurous young men surely chose a spot to cross it where the bank was less steep and the river narrow enough to swim. It is easy to imagine them alert, discreet, their robes clinging about their strong limbs as they pressed on with quick steps the last few miles to the key city of the plain. Eager to avoid identity, they mixed only briefly with the crowds outside the city. Just long enough, perhaps, to hear that the house situated so strategically on the walls belonged to a harlot named Rahab. Here they found at least a measure of safety, for city authorities had likely often seen strangers enter her home.

The Believer

The strange and somewhat romantic story of Rahab presents many moral difficulties. It is easy to see that men of sterling character and exemplary lives like Abraham, the friend of God, and Moses, the servant of Jehovah, belong among the heroes of faith. But it is hard for many to see that Rahab, with her pagan heritage and her questionable morals, belongs in that illustrious line of men and women whose faith we must emulate. Commentators have tried to explain away the blot of prostitution from Christ's lineage by insisting that in those days a harlot was actually only an inn-keeper. Others say she may have fallen into sin once but now was respectable. But the truth cannot be evaded, for we find that she is everywhere called a harlot. The ways of the Lord are past finding

out—"so are my ways higher than your ways, and my thoughts
than your thoughts" (Isa. 55:9).

> The dark threads are as needful
> In the weaver's skillful hand,
> As the threads of gold and silver,
> For the pattern which He planned.
> —Author Unknown

In Matthew 1:5, we find that among the four women named in
the messianic line, one of whom is Rahab, three are adulteresses.
The Lord is telling us that salvation is not dependent on human
goodness but on His free grace to sinners and that He is willing to
redeem the most sinful. This example of how He elevated a sinful
woman warns us that we may never look down with disdain upon
others because of their sins.

We have evidence that Rahab lied and did so very cleverly. A lie
meant very little to the depraved Canaanites but is always a sin in
the ears of God. And who is more despicable than a traitor? She
knew that the spies had come to check on the fortifications of the
city and to determine the morale of the people. She had freely told
them all she knew. She had encouraged them, protected them, and
helped them escape. Rahab could have done no more to betray her
friends and her country.

Yet, Rahab, the harlot, the clever liar, the traitor, became a heroine of faith! She spared the spies and was later saved herself because she *truly believed* in God. She told the men that she had heard
about God before. Jericho was on a caravan route from Babylon to
Egypt and, considering that traveling merchants stopped at such
houses as hers, she may have heard much about this growing nation, their conquests, and the power of their God. Her people were
overcome with fear of a god so great as the I AM of the Israelites, but
she believed that this must be the one true God. God had been
working in her heart. There is conviction in her confession, "I know
that the LORD hath given . . . the LORD dried up the water of the Red

sea . . . he is God in heaven above, and in earth beneath" (Josh. 2:9–11). There is no room left anywhere in her mind for Ashteroth, Baal, or Moloch!

The Insider

Rahab and Sarah are the only women named in that great cloud of witnesses who were strangers and pilgrims on the earth and for whom God prepared a city. In James, we find Rahab's faith is placed alongside that of the eminent Abraham. James says that her faith was living, for it was proved by her works. Her convictions were sure and, even though her life was endangered by doing so, she chose God's side. She dared to stand alone, for she knew that she was secure with the Almighty. She helped the spies and kept their secret for God's sake. See how quickly she thought of the welfare of her family! She was already a missionary, shall we say, for she wanted them to be saved also. "For as the body without the spirit is dead, so faith without works is dead also" (James 2:26). That is the lesson of Rahab!

She and her family were saved from the horrible destruction of the city, and her own reward was eternal. So we see that every kind action done for the love of God and Christ will be repaid a thousandfold. Even the "cup of cold water" does not lose its reward! She was taken into the fellowship of the Israelites and became one of them. It appears that she married Salmon, who may have been one of the two spies. Their son Boaz married Ruth, and they were the grandparents of David. Christ is still seeking and saving the lost, and He is calling not the righteous but sinners to repentance. He is the Good Shepherd who brings the lost and the straying of every people into the fold.

The church has been slow to make the "outsider" an insider, slow to learn and practice the principle of acceptance. No one of a different heritage, color, or culture—no kind of sinner who has accepted Christ—may be kept out. When God saves sinners, no matter how wretched, He takes them *completely* into His fellowship and into His heaven. Whether their heritage is Reformed or pagan, their nationality Dutch or African-American, makes no difference to God. When the chief priest and elders, who were steeped in "background" and tradition, questioned Jesus, He said, "Verily I say unto you, That the publicans and the harlots go into the kingdom of God before you" (Matt. 21:31). The deeper the need, the greater the grace. All glory to Him who saves to the uttermost!

Suggestions for Discussion

1. From whom were the Canaanites descendants (Gen. 9:18)? Why did God destroy them?
2. How would Israel be punished if that nation forgot God (Deut. 8:19–20)?
3. What do we know of the material resources and blessings of the land of Canaan (Deut. 8:7–10)?
4. How do we know that the land of the Phoenicians or Canaanites was divided into states or kingdoms (Josh. 9:1–2)?
5. Was it necessary for Joshua to make detailed plans to take the land after the Lord already had promised to *give* the land to Israel? Recount what you can of the strategy Joshua used. Do you think his methods have any similarity to those used in present-day warfare?
6. Tell what you can about Rahab's background and life. How much did she know about God before the spies came?
7. Show that Rahab had faith. What kind of faith did she have?
8. Why do we do good works? Must it be a *conscious* doing or a natural outcome of faith?
9. Is there any symbolism in the scarlet thread that Rahab hung from the window?
10. Does the story of Rahab shed any light on what our attitude should be toward converts? What is our present-day attitude toward them? What should it be?

11. We occasionally have outsiders come into our church. Do we really take in the Rahabs? What did Jesus do?

12. Do you think the church should accept a sincere convert who has, previous to conversion, been divorced on unbiblical grounds?

Awake, awake, Deborah: awake, awake, utter a song.
—Judges 5:12

12

Deborah

Scripture Reading
Judges 4–5

Women have been in the news now for more than a hundred years. A certain writer is convinced that the greatest fact of this century is not the great world wars that we have lived through, but woman.

In *Angels and Amazons,* written by Inez Irwin, we read that women had more rights, in some respects, in colonial days than in the early Republic. In the nineteenth century, a movement was spearheaded to give women equal rights with men. This feminist movement first impressed itself on the public mind as a series of claims to equal citizenship in politics, education, industrial employment, legal status, and social respect. Such women as Abigail Adams, Susan B. Anthony, and Lucretia Mott were leaders among the many who fought the "Hundred Years' War for Women's Self-Determination," as it was called. This struggle reached something of a conclusion with the war of 1914, after which the *new woman* appeared, demonstrating she had equal rights with man in nearly every field.

The struggle for equal opportunities and equal pay, however, has not been wholly successful. In *Ladies of Courage,* by L. A. Hickok and Eleanor Roosevelt, we are told that the Nineteenth Amendment, which gives women the right to vote, also gives her equal rights to hold office, even that of the highest in the land. Woman has only begun to appropriate these rights. Material in the public libraries on famous women today is scarce and not very impressive. Jacqueline Kennedy, the nation's thirty-first First Lady, was apolitical and made her impact in style, taste, and personality. The political campaign of Governor Lurleen Wallace of Alabama was a husband-wife affair and, during her term in office, she did not swerve from the policies of her husband. Worldwide, Indira Gandhi and Margaret Thatcher have both headed governments. The *new woman* is here to stay.

When we study Deborah, we conclude that there is nothing new under the sun, for there were also *new women* in early civilization. The heroic, gifted, public-minded Deborah was a new woman in an age that is very old. Although we might still agree that women's greatest sphere of power is in the home, God does endow some women with superior gifts and, for such women as Deborah, even men will step aside or follow in her train.

"Awake, Deborah"

"For who is God, save the LORD? and who is a rock, save our God?" (2 Sam. 22:32) was the confession of David, the king. He knew that the God of the Covenant was not subject to even the shadow of inconstancy. Few nations had more ups and downs, spiritually and nationally, than His chosen people—but the holy and immutable God does not waver, even where His chosen people are concerned.

God had said, "All this land will I give you . . . and I will never break my covenant with you." God promised to destroy the nations in Canaan, but Israel had to dispossess them (Deut. 31:3). They were told to break down the altars of the heathen and make no covenant with them. They were forbidden to intermarry with the people of the land. Israel was to have nothing to do with these nations; they were not even to name their gods (Josh. 23:7; Judg. 2:2).

The people, deeply impressed, said, "God forbid that we should forsake the LORD, to serve other gods" (Josh. 24:16). How positive they were: "Nay, but we will serve Jehovah." But how soon their ardor cooled! They were hardly settled in the land when they proved to be greedy, selfish, and forgetful of Him from whom all blessings flowed. They took God's earthly gifts but rejected His Word. God's purpose was the destruction of idolatry, but theirs became the enjoyment of their vineyards and the mixing of cultures. In spite of pious promises, the Israelites turned their backs on God and became carnal and increasingly corrupt, becoming friends with the sensual Canaanites and bowing down to their idols (Judg. 2; 3:5–7).

Then the anger of the Lord burned against the children of Israel and, wherever they went, the hand of Jehovah was against them for evil. God's promises to His people are sure, but He cannot condone disobedience and evil. His hate of sin is as certain as His marvelous display of grace. God's people had forsaken Him, and now He would no longer help them to drive out the rest of the Canaanites. Many heathen nations would now remain in the land (which they could have possessed completely), and these people would be like unrelenting thorns in their sides. Their gods would be snares to them. Distressed as Israel became, they had no excuse for their predicament, for Jehovah had warned them repeatedly and had reasoned with them, "Why have ye done this?" With their lips they said, "We will serve Jehovah," but they bowed in the dust before Baal and gave the strength of their bodies to Ashteroth. How like God's ancient children we are! We say, "Use me for Thy glory," and then seek our own. We pray, "Help me to live for Thee," and then spend all of our strength to satisfy selfish desires.

We read that God sold the nation to their enemies, as if to say, "They are not Mine, they are yours; do with them as you will" (Josh. 23:13; Judg. 4:2). So Israel was exploited and burdened; their crops were eaten by another, their property pillaged. People were turned out of their homes, their women were molested, and their young men were made slaves. Warriors were cowed and leaders dispersed. They were in extreme distress. Independence was gone, and they were oppressed by a strong military power with no sense of justice. This time it was Jabin, the king of Canaan, and ruthless Sisera, who held them in iron clutches.

At last, there was no way for this stiff-necked people to look but up. They cried out to God, and He heard and provided a deliverer, the strong-minded Deborah. It was in her ear that they poured out their troubles. They knew her to be a courageous, wise, and godly woman, and they cried, "Awake, awake, Deborah: awake, awake, utter a song" (Judg. 5:12), hoping that, though they were sore distressed and deeply humbled, they would once again come to sing the glorious praises of the great I AM.

"I Deborah Arose"'

This strong and courageous woman became Israel's Joan of Arc, routing the enemy and restoring freedom. But long before she became great in war, she was a homemaker, a mother in Israel. She had a heart touched with compassion, not only for her family but for all of Israel. She had heard of, and perhaps even seen, the atrocities her people had endured for a long twenty years. Their suffering brought her to her knees before the living Jehovah, in whom she had implicit faith. It is said that all true prayer is dangerous, because it calls for the giving of self. Is it not true that the more we pray, the more earnest we become, and the more willing we are to do His will?

As a prophetess, she talked to her fainthearted people about God and His power to help. She predicted deliverance if they would only turn back to Him. This is always the first step toward peace for us too, no matter what our problem may be.

This was not the first time Israel had been in trouble. After Joshua's death, they had often fallen into sin, suffered for it, and mercifully been delivered by Spirit-filled men called judges. This high honor was now given to Deborah. She became well known throughout the country. People came from far and near to the place where she held court—under a stately palm tree, itself a symbol of prosperity and victory. She had a real task because of the widespread rejection of God and because "every man did that which was right in his own eyes" (Judg. 17:6). As a judge and prophetess, she was an inspired woman. People who came to her for counsel, instruction, and comfort left filled with hope for a better day.

She could do more than judge and prophesy. She could stir up the people. This noble woman must have had a sparkling, magnetic personality and, surely, a dauntless spirit. We can be certain that she was an eloquent agitator to be able to stir up such a broken and despairing people. How wonderful that she could inspire others with the same trust in God that she had. She became great because she saw a need and did something about it. She said, "[The rulers] ceased in Israel, until that I Deborah arose . . . a mother in Israel" (Judg. 5:7). And she "mothered" her people well, for the land had rest for forty years.

"My Soul, March On"

It has been said that women in politics must not look for honor or merely desire to have a voice in government. They must have devotion to a purpose. This Deborah had. She set her determined face to the goal of freedom. She called a warrior, General Barak from Kedesh-Naphtali, and said that he must go and fight as God had commanded, and He would give victory. Barak's faith was weak. He would go only if Deborah went along. She said, "I will surely go with thee."

In the verses that follow, we read an account of one of the most remarkable battles in history. Many rallied to the call to arms, but not all. There were isolationists in Israel. Meroz was unpatriotic. Some of the tribes were so deeply concerned about their farms and businesses (Judg. 5:16–17) that, though they *considered* the nation's peril, they did not come to help. They were cursed for this. Ten thousand valiant men came from Zebulon, Naphtali, and Issachar. They marched up to the top of Mount Tabor with Deborah to inspire them and Barak to lead them into battle. From this lofty vantage point, there was a grand panoramic view of central Palestine. There on the Plain of Esdraelon plunged the broad Kishon, fed by many rivulets and springs that, during the winter rains, made the marshes and valley treacherous.

They saw the host of Sisera, with his nine hundred chariots of iron, pitched in the valley. Though they had inadequate equipment, they arose as one when Deborah shouted, "Up; for this is the day . . . is not the LORD gone out before thee?" (Judg. 4:14). God fought for them by sending torrents of rain and earthquakes to confuse Sisera and his hosts. Chariots were bogged down in mire and weeds. The swollen Kishon swept hundreds away. Barak's men attacked fearlessly and furiously until not a man was left but Sisera, who escaped on foot to the hill country where the Kenites lived. In the friendly tent of Jael and Heber, he was felled and lay "pierced and stricken through his temples" (Judg. 5:26). So the mighty Sisera died. The song of Deborah, which she wrote and sang with Barak, is one of wonderful beauty and lyric power. In it, she praises the faithful warrior but, most of all, she exults in God and gives Him the praise for the victory.

May we, like Deborah, *awaken* to the need of the kingdom of God, *arise* to do our part, and *march* on with the Lord of Hosts to victory. And those who love and serve Him will "be as the sun when he goeth forth in his might" (Judg. 5:31).

Suggestions for Discussion

1. Where did Deborah live? Who was her husband? Where did she sit to judge?
2. Name several things Deborah did well.
3. How many judges preceded Deborah? Name them.
4. If a woman had the right to prophesy under the old

dispensation, may she not have the right to preach under the present?

5. How would you describe Deborah's personality?

6. Which heathen nations became thorns in the side of the children of Israel (Judg. 3:1–5)?

7. What tribes answered the call to duty? Who stayed at home and why? See Judges 5.

8. Is there room for conscientious objectors in times of war?

9. Who were the Kenites? Where were their sympathies?

10. Describe the famous battle between Israel and Sisera.

11. Is there a spiritual meaning for us in this story of Deborah?

12. Are we, as women, taking a sufficiently active part in political life? What are some of the things that women can do in this field?

Thy daughter-in-law, which loveth thee, . . . is better
to thee than seven sons.
—Ruth 4:15

13

Naomi

Scripture Reading
The Book of Ruth

The setting of our story is the land of Moab. The father of the Moabites was Lot's son by his eldest daughter, and he lived in the vicinity of Zoar. The Ammonites, also from Lot, went to the northeast; but the more peaceful Moabites remained nearer home, replacing the tall and mighty Emims. The territory, east of the Dead Sea and opposite Jericho, had been given by God to the children of Lot for a possession. When Moses led the Israelites to Canaan they did not invade Moab, because God had told them not to vex them or fight against them. The Moabites, though they did not allow Israel to pass through their land, were friendly to them.

It appears that they were not a hostile people, for Jephthah says that Moab did not fight against Israel when they were neighbors for some three hundred years. There were, however, times when Moab and Israel clashed. Because Israel did evil, God strengthened Moab to oppress His people for eighteen years. Ehud freed Israel. David laid tribute on Moab. The Moabites were subject to Israel's Omri, but when Ahab died, they revolted. We read that years later bands of Moabites harassed Judah, yet during the Babylonian captivity many Jews found refuge in Moab.

Isaiah prophesied that, in the end, Moab would be cursed to desolation by Jehovah because of her pride and arrogance. Nevertheless, Jeremiah, who was acquainted with Israel's prophecy, promised a gleam of hope for the Moabites.

This was the nation whose people befriended Naomi and her family when they found a temporary residence among them.

"Call Me Mara"

In this much-loved book, we are led aside from the highway of Hebrew history, with its heroism, violence, and wars, into a beautiful by-path of domestic life. It is a story of love, anxiety, sorrow, and sweetness, and it fills the human heart. The book is called Ruth, but without Naomi there would be no Ruth. There are few narratives as touchingly beautiful as this about Naomi. Through adversity, she discovered that God is good, kind, and merciful to the afflicted.

Naomi was fortunate in that her husband's inheritance lay in the fertile fields of Bethlehem. From early history, the lush valley that sloped from the hilltop city to the north, south, and east had been so exceptionally productive that the city that overlooked the terraced expanse of grain and fruits was called the House of Bread.

Now the unexpected happened. There was dire famine in the land! Elimelech's fertile fields lay stripped and desolate. Poverty and hunger prevailed. Some believe that the famine was occasioned by an invasion of enemies who came like a multitude of locusts to destroy the land (Judg. 6:1– 6). Elimelech was desperate; he could not keep the wolf of hunger from the door.

Naomi and Elimelech faced a serious problem. They heard that in the land of Moab there was plenty to eat, and Moab was not far away. From the hills around Bethlehem, across the narrow thread of the Jordan and the hazy expanse of the Dead Sea, they could see the purple mountains of Moab. It was hard for Naomi to consent to go; home and friends and many little things mean so much to a woman. Nevertheless, contemplating the dry stubble of her garden and the thin forms of her lads, she knew she had no choice.

Elimelech, whose name means "God is King," did what little he could to make his modest inheritance secure. He gathered his remaining cattle, his simple possessions, and his family and set out. For the boys, the dusty trail to Moab was the highway to adventure. It must have been hardest for Naomi to break ties with friends and relatives and to turn from familiar scenes, for she had a loving and sensitive heart.

We conclude that this needy little family was cordially received in Moab. The language of Moab was much the same as theirs, and the boys soon made friends among the Moabites. However, Naomi and Elimelech must have been deeply concerned when Mahlon and Chilion became seriously interested in the girls of the land. Although there had been no definite pronouncement against marriage with the Moabites, both parents must have been concerned, for they had known of many fine Hebrew boys who had married Moabite maidens and then had turned to Chemosh, the god of Moab.

They had only been in Moab a short time when God took Elimelech from the side of Naomi. Now the burden of support and family problems rested solely on her slim shoulders. She was a widow—a somber fact in itself. Her loneliness was doubled in that she was so far from home, family, and friends. She found that, though children are a blessing, they are also a grave responsibility. How her heart must have ached for them with their needs and problems!

Here, in the valley of Moab, where Israel had wept for thirty days for Moses, Naomi cried piteously that Jehovah might lift her up and make her wise and strong for life. God assured her:

> I know thy sorrow, child; I know it well
> Thou need'st not try with broken voice to tell
> Just let me lay thy head here on my breast,
> And find here sweetest comfort, perfect rest.
> —Author Unknown

And Naomi learned, day by day, that Jehovah was her refuge and strength, that He was the Father of mercies and the God of all comfort.

When Mahlon and Chilion grew up, they married Ruth and Orpah—both, Moabitish girls. Naomi must have been hurt and dismayed by her sons' marriages with heathen girls, but she had the grace and good sense to take them into her home and heart. Often, the advice of parents goes by the board, especially if their young sons and daughters are in love. When children make what seem to be foolish or unsuitable marriages, parents may be so emotion-impelled that they speak rashly—and that is the surest way to lose those children. Naomi knew that to save both her sons and their wives she must make the girls welcome and love them.

After a few years, Mahlon and Chilion also became ill and died. Naomi had expected to find support from them and a reason for living. In the space of about ten years, three of the little pilgrim family of four had been laid to rest. Now she was a childless widow in a strange land. She had left Bethlehem young, happy, and "full," and now she was "empty" of all but sorrow and sadness. She could surely say, "All thy waves and thy billows are gone over me" (Ps. 42:7).

> Child of my love, lean hard,
> And let me feel the pressure of thy cares;
> I know thy burden child, I shaped it.
> —Paul Pastnor

"God Is Sweet"

We all know people who are pressed down with sorrow and hardship, and whose lives need the sweetness of love and friendship. As Christians, we must bear one another's burdens and so fulfill the law of Christ. Those who are prosperous often stay cruelly distant from widows and their children. Ready with advice, but doing nothing to cheer or lighten the load, these people are apt to say, "There is really so little we can do." Widows do not need pity, but they do long for love and understanding.

God was loving Naomi all the while that He was leading her through the shadows. The eternal Father, drawing her close to the shoulder of His love, whispered to her heart, "Believe me, child, all things do work together for good to those who love Me. Trust Me. Though you may be pressed almost unendurably—yet My grace is sufficient for you."

Tired and old, Naomi yearned for her kindred and the home of her youth. When she heard that Jehovah had visited His people to give them bread again, she determined to go back to Bethlehem. We admire her because, no matter how low her circumstances were, her fine womanly independence remained, and she had the courage to face life alone with God.

She and her daughters-in-law were three widows united by the bond of affliction. Now she urged them to seek happiness anew where they could best find it—in their own land. "The LORD deal kindly" (Ruth 1:8). Ah! Naomi *knew* the Lord. Do we believe that the Lord deals *kindly* when everything seems to go wrong? Walking toward Bethlehem with her daughters-in-law at her side, she recalled days gone by in Moab. Trembling with emotion, she told them how she loved them and thanked them for the kindness they had shown to her family. How could they help but love this dear woman who had faced overwhelming adversity with a gentle and submissive spirit.

Orpah returned to her heathen home, but Ruth could not tear herself from the embrace of her mother-in-law. Naomi had a God-possessed personality. She had a sweetness that completely won Ruth. Ruth needed her; she needed the God who upheld Naomi. Because Naomi was true to God in the stress and storm of life, a beautiful thing happened. She won Ruth for God, and no confession of love has ever surpassed that of Ruth, the daughter-in-law, to her mother-in-law.

So the two went on until they came to Bethlehem. It was harvest time, and never had the fields been more inviting or the flowers smelled so sweet. How the little white houses gleamed in the sun! Dusty and tired, deep lines of sorrow and suffering etching her face,

Naomi was hardly recognized by old friends. "Is *this* Naomi?" they asked one another. There was much ado in the little town for many days—and Naomi had much to tell. Her mother had named her Naomi, "God is sweet," for He had been sweet in His dealing with her. But Naomi said, "Call me Mara: for the Almighty hath dealt very bitterly with me. I went out full, and the LORD hath brought me home again empty" (Ruth 1:20–21). Nevertheless, we can learn from Naomi.

> For the Lord Himself had said it
> He, the faithful God and True;
> When thou comest to the waters
> Thou shalt not go down, but through.
> —Annie Johnson Flint

She did not become useless with self-pity. She testified to her friends that Jehovah was the Lord of her life. She had lived in a heathen land so devoutly that Ruth could say, "Thy God [shall be] my God" (Ruth 1:16). At home again, she counseled Ruth and planned for her so that her life might be full and secure. Ruth married the man Naomi approved of, and Ruth was better to her than seven sons—so the women, Naomi's neighbors, said. They praised God when Naomi's grandson was born. "There is a son born to Naomi" (Ruth 4:17) said these women, and they named him Obed.

Yes, for every trial there is sweet compensation. God takes away that He may give Himself to us the more abundantly. Jesus does not show His love to us preventing our suffering but by making us strong enough to endure. He shows His love by purifying and molding our characters until the beauty of Jesus is seen in us.

> God means it unto good for thee, dear friend
> The God of Naomi is the same today;
> His love permits afflictions strange and bitter,
> His hand is guiding through the unknown way.
> —Author Unknown

Suggestions for Discussion

1. To follow the brief story of Moab as given in the introduction look up the following:
    a. Genesis 19:36–37
    b. Deuteronomy 2:9, 28–29
    c. Judges 3:12–30; 11:17, 25–26
    d. 2 Kings 3:4–5
    e. Isaiah 15–16
    f. Jeremiah 40:11–12
2. What do we learn about Moab in Isaiah 15–16 and Jeremiah 48:46–47?
3. Why did Naomi and Elimelech go to Moab?
4. How was Naomi afflicted?
5. Was it right for Naomi to say "the Almighty hath dealt very bitterly with me" (Ruth 1:20)?
6. Widows often say they feel like a "fifth wheel" in mixed company. Would it be best for them to fellowship mainly with other women who understand them and their problems? Discuss this problem. It may be helpful to some in your group.
7. Read James 1:27. What does this verse mean?
8. What should a widow's attitude be toward receiving help from the church?
9. How does self-pity usually affect a person?
10. What makes Naomi an example in time of trouble?
11. Why is Naomi an exemplary mother-in-law?

Thy people shall be my people, and thy God my God.
—Ruth 1:16

14

ℛuth

Scripture Reading
Deuteronomy 25:5–10; The Book of Ruth;
Matthew 1:5–6

The historical novel is always extremely popular, and when it has a biblical background it carries a special appeal to many people. Such books as *The Robe* and *The Big Fisherman,* both by Douglas; *The Galilean* by Slaughter; *The Cardinal* by Robinson; and *The Prophet* by Asch, to mention a few, seldom lay on the library shelf. Why do you suppose that these books are so popular?

Many books have been written about Ruth throughout the years. When we asked our librarian for the newest ones she said, "I hardly need to look for them. They are so much in demand that they are almost never in." There is Frank Slaughter's novel *The Song of Ruth,* and others, such as, *The Song of the Cave* by Murphy, and *Ruth* by Fineman. Though there is much that is not elevating in these stories, we do recognize the attempt of the authors to produce some good thoughts, while making one of the oldest and most touching love stories in the world come to life again.

More satisfying to the serious Bible student are the nonfiction books and stories on Ruth by Knight, Taylor, Deen, Lofts, and others. These, as well as novels written about Ruth, will always carry a great appeal, for they tell the story of the beautiful romance of the Moabitish maiden who linked, by pure devotion, the Gentile world with the people of God.

The Ideal Young Widow

The book of Ruth is a gem among the books of the Old Testament. It is placed correctly between Judges and Samuel, for Naomi and Ruth lived in the time of the Judges. The book itself is considered to have been written at a much later date. It is beautifully and simply written. Goethe, the German poet, says that it is "the loveliest little idyll that tradition has transmitted to us." It is a true story of loyalty and devotion to one's family. It brings a vital message to us who live in a modern age with its serious family problems.

Ruth, the central figure in this book, is one of the best-known women in the Bible. The world would not consider her spectacular or heroic. She is unusual only in her own sense of loyalty and devotion to her mother-in-law and to her adopted people. H. Morton says, "Ruth's outstanding quality was a beauty of heart, a generosity of soul, a firm sense of duty, and a meekness which often goes hand in hand with decision." She always seemed to say and do the right thing in a charming way.

The Bible does not describe her appearance, but literature and art have made her extremely lovely. In *The Song of Ruth,* she is pictured as being "startlingly beautiful, with dark red hair, high cheekbones, warm eyes, and dressed in the clinging robes of a temple priestess." Actually, it is the appeal of her lovely character that causes us to draw a beautiful picture of Ruth, the Moabitess.

We are first introduced to Ruth when, as a young widow, she faces an uncertain future. The ten happy years of her marriage had passed all too swiftly. She had met Mahlon, a young Jew, when he had come to the fertile highlands of Moab with his parents to stay until the famine in Judah was over. Mahlon and Ruth had fallen in love and were married. They were happy, but—a woman needs a child to love and a man needs a son beside him. It was a crushing blow to lose Mahlon, but she found comfort and understanding in her noble and wonderful mother-in-law, Naomi. The problem they faced together was real, for an "empty" widow could find "rest" and security only in the house of her husband.

Naomi resolutely faced the fate of a widow in the Eastern family and decided to go back to her old home and relatives. Ruth and Orpah started out with her for Bethlehem. On the way Naomi urged the girls to return to Moab and marry again. Orpah turned back but Ruth was reluctant to part. She adored Naomi, the perfect wife and mother, calm and courageous in the face of adversity. In Ruth's response (Ruth 1:16–17) we hear the most exquisite expression of love and devotion in the whole of literature. Never has devotion been more perfectly expressed or been more self-forgetting.

Ruth proved to be a woman of decision. Though Naomi had said that she could offer her nothing a woman needs in Judah, Ruth firmly closed the door to her way of life, her family, and her gods and bravely faced a bleak and uncertain future by the side of her destitute mother-in-law.

It was springtime when the two widows slowly walked, or perhaps rode their donkeys, along the narrow, dusty road toward home. The one, old and withered, in a black *malaaya;* the other, young with golden amulets gleaming beneath the head cloth on her lovely brow and the spring breeze fluttering her long gown. We can be sure that Naomi's talk was about the people and the God whom Ruth had chosen for her own. It was the middle of April—wild blue iris, anemones, and poppies bloomed in cheerful profusion along the path and on the hillsides. Bethlehem's fields of golden grain swayed under the warm eastern sun. As the women climbed the sharp trail to the city, they saw the bright fields dotted with reapers—men and women—cutting the ripe grain with sickles, binding, and happily gathering the harvest. In the city Naomi was welcomed by the people.

The Ideal Daughter-in-Law

Ruth now became Naomi's means of support. Each family usually had sufficient women to care for the complete needs of the household. There was no work for a woman outside of the home. The poor and the widow would have been destitute, indeed, if God had not provided for them (Lev. 19:9–10). To be a gleaner with the other poor was a humble task. Ruth was not afraid of work (Ruth 2:7) and gleaned from the break of day until the warm red sun left its last glow on the swaying barley and slowly dipped behind the low hills of Judah. After beating the precious grain from the stalks, she filled her shawl with the barley and went home to waiting Naomi.

The fields were one wide stretch of corn and grain, marked only by heaps of stones that were the landmarks. Ruth did not know to whom the field belonged until, after she had courteously asked permission to glean, she was told that this great plot belonged to Boaz, a rich landowner who was wise, generous, influential, and highly respected in the community. When Boaz came out to his acres to see how the harvest was progressing, he saw the attractive strange girl among the reapers. He spoke kindly to her and invited her to glean in his fields throughout the harvest. She, with his maidens, followed the reapers several weeks. Boaz admired the quiet loveliness of Ruth, her industry, courtesy, and devotion. He showed her special consideration, for which she was grateful (Ruth 2:10, 13).

Family Ideals

Naomi was happy that Boaz showed such interest in Ruth, for he was a near kinsman. A plan began to form in her mind for she saw a way of preserving the family name and making Ruth happy at the same time.

The family unit was basic in Naomi's day. It was all-important to maintain the family name and estate through the generations. In the event of the father's death, the oldest son took over the family property and also the support of the women in the family. If a man died without an heir, the Levirate law required a brother to marry the widow. The first son then became the legal heir of the deceased man, so continuing his name and inheriting his property. The entire family lived on the estate and worked together to provide for all the family needs.

There have been tremendous changes in family patterns in modern times. The idea that the birth of children is an act of God has long since given way to planning for as few children as parents can comfortably support and care for. The American family consists of independents using the home mainly for a place to sleep, eat, and hang their hats.

The traditional compact home unit has disintegrated to the degree that marriages are often in serious trouble. Parents yield control over their children to various outside influences. Solutions to home and juvenile difficulties are constantly being offered, but problems continue to grow. The Christian parents' task in this changing world is to build a solid family unit in which there is mutual love and devotion.

An Ideal Marriage

Naomi, delighted with Boaz's attentions to Ruth, plans a brighter future for her. She tells Ruth of the Levirate law and wants her to claim its benefits. Naomi, courageous and wise, tells Ruth what to do and say. Ruth, trusting and dutiful, says, "All that thou sayest unto me I will do" (Ruth 3:5).

Boaz had seen Ruth in coarse work clothes—now he must see her in all her sweet loveliness, properly robed and fragrant. Veiling her face, she goes into the falling night. She is guided by the light of the round harvest moon that hangs in golden splendor over the Judean hills. Going to the threshing floor she steps softly between the heavily breathing men with their cloaks wrapped about them to where Boaz lies sleeping. It was a strange old custom that Ruth employed to make this legal call. Boaz receives her courteously, tells her that he admires her, and they talk of marriage (Ruth 3:10–14). But, he must first consult the nearer kinsman.

We see Boaz, early at the city gate, capably negotiating for Naomi and Ruth. The nearer kinsman cannot afford to redeem both the property and Ruth, after which Boaz publicly announces his intentions to marry Ruth. The elders and the many people who are present are happy with the outcome, for they respect the noble Boaz and have heard only good about the lovely Moabitess. Many are the good wishes and blessings showered upon the bride and groom. So Boaz redeemed Ruth into the family of God's people, and her desire to be one with them in faith and fellowship was realized.

Soon a son, Obed, was born. All who knew Naomi, Ruth, and Boaz were glad and said, "Blessed be the LORD" (Ruth 4:14). Obed became famous in Israel, for he was the grandfather of David from whose house and lineage Christ the Redeemer was born. So Ruth, the Moabitess with the beautiful character, was linked with the Son of David, who was the True Light to the Gentiles, and with all the redeemed from the ends of the earth.

Suggestions for Discussion

1. What does the name Ruth mean? Compare it with the meaning of the word *ruthless*. Characterize Ruth.
2. Was it love for God or for Naomi that determined Ruth's choice?
3. In case of financial need in the family circle, whose duty do you think it is to help: family members, the church, or the state?
4. What special provision was made for the poor among the Israelites?
5. Notice the greetings used (Ruth 2:4). Were the Israelites more God-conscious than we are?
6. Compare family patterns in Ruth's day and ours. What changes have come even since our grandparents' day? Have these changes helped family relations?

7. What is the reason there is so much divorce? For the problems schools have with children these days? What solutions would you offer if you were asked to help solve these problems?

8. Tell the story of Naomi's matchmaking, paying special attention to her womanly wisdom.

9. Should a woman maneuver to get the man she wants, or is it really up to the man to choose a spouse?

10. What are the main values shown in the book of Ruth?

*For this child I prayed; and the L*ORD *hath given me my petition.*
—1 Samuel 1:27

15

Hannah

Scripture Reading
1 Samuel 1–2

$\mathscr{W}$e believe that prayer is a great reality—that prayer changes things. It is the Christian's vital breath and native air. We know that He who taught His disciples to pray can teach us how to pray.

Prayer is power. We as Christians have the tremendous possibility of speaking personally with the Supreme Power who directs our lives and the destiny of all things. When we, in our deep need, come into vital contact with God's might and mercy, things are bound to change.

Prayer is self discipline, and Christian character grows in the secret place of prayer.

We bring our needs before our Father and He answers us. He makes things happen for us. Jesus says, "If ye have faith as a grain of mustard seed, ye shall say unto this mountain, Remove hence to yonder place; and it shall remove" (Matt. 17:20).

In the Psalms, we have many promises that God hears and

answers prayer: "This poor man cried, and the LORD heard him, and saved him out of all his troubles" (Ps. 34:6). We find many examples of definite answers to prayer in the Old Testament. The story of Hannah is a positive proof of the power of prayer, for Hannah's prayer took hold of God's mercy and He gave her the desire of her heart (1 Sam. 1:27).

Hannah's Problem

Hannah was the mother of Samuel, who was the first great prophet after Moses and the last of the judges, the founder of the School of Prophets and of the Hebrew Monarchy. Two Bible books are named after him, the first of which gives an account of his life and labors. Hannah had a worthy son, but she was also a worthy mother. She represents the ideal in godly motherhood—humble, consecrated, and loyal.

We admire her humility and piety all the more when we think of the daily trials that were hers. Many a woman in her position would have become bitter, but she became a better child of God as she was driven close to the One who alone understood.

Hannah's husband, Elkanah, was of the house of Levi. He was a good man. Each year he religiously went to Shiloh to keep the feast. The people were in a state of moral decay, and the high ideals of Moses were all but forgotten. Many of the judges, like Samson, were poor leaders. Fearful crimes were being committed and horrible retaliations took place (Judg. 19–20). Each man made laws to suit his own needs (Judg. 21:25). The times were not conducive to godliness or to worship, but Elkanah never missed the feast at Shiloh. He is to be commended for taking his family to worship—even though it was a ten-mile walk to Shiloh from where they lived in the hills of Ephraim. He taught his children to worship and sacrifice to the Lord of Hosts, and he knew who the Lord was (Exod. 34:6–7).

Yet this good man had serious family troubles. It was Elkanah's own sin that brought about friction in his otherwise model family. Elkanah practiced polygamy—he had two wives.

This practice was widespread and is reported, without embarrassment, of some of the greatest of the Old Testament figures: patriarchs, judges, and kings. It was practiced among the wealthy and the middle class, to which Elkanah belonged. Extra wives were taken for various reasons: occasionally for political alliance; often for lust; sometimes to take in the single woman, for there was no place for them in Hebrew society; and for economic purposes. The most important reason for polygamy was the survival of the family. Wives were a means of securing children. When the first wife was barren, a second was often taken. The strong probability is that Hannah was his first wife and, being childless, he married Peninnah for children. The practice of polygamy was taken over from a heathen culture for, in the beginning, God instituted monogamous marriage.

So Elkanah, as he went to Shiloh each year, carried a sin in his heart, a sin which multiplied into many family sins, and he did nothing to eradicate it. His story is timely, for many of us continue to go piously up to God's house week after week harboring wrongs that we tolerate and even excuse.

Peninnah, inferior in character and, consequently, not as able a woman as Hannah, gave Elkanah the children he desired. It was only natural that Hannah's sterility brought her desperate anxiety, for her honor and worth as a woman was contingent on bearing a son. Even the grief of Jepthah's daughter was found not so much in the rash vow of her father as in her inability to fulfill her womanhood (Judg. 11:37). Hannah's frustration and grief were intensified by Peninnah's persistent unkind attitude and expressions. The cruel jibes and jeers of her rival were agony to the gentle spirit of Hannah. Little did Peninnah realize that she was sinning against God by grieving Hannah, by hurting her husband, and by setting a bad example for her children. The "Peninnah-spirit" is found everywhere—it is only too common among us. The antidote is love. He who loves God must love his brother also.

This shepherd family must have looked forward to this once-a-year trip to the feast at Shiloh. Though Hannah was Elkanah's favorite wife, even this happy festival became a trial for her. To see parents and children coming together to the feast year after year made her realize the more poignantly that she had no part in the coming generation. To see Elkanah's pride in his children as he handed each their portion at the feast made her feel that as much as her husband loved her, she missed the most precious gift that life can give. Elkanah was a sympathetic person and tenderly tried to comfort her. But there was no comfort in the extra portion Elkanah gave her, for the dark eyes of Peninnah were always watchful, smoldering with resentment and hate. Peninnah saw that Hannah was loved, and it impelled her to meanness. The inevitable result of polygamous marriage was always jealousy, hate, and rivalry (e.g., Deut. 21:15–17). However, the bitterness of such an atmosphere, from which Hannah could not for even a day escape, drove her not to angry retorts but to the inner chamber of prayer.

Hannah's Prayer

This feast day Peninnah's gloating was detestable, her jibes were agonizing (1 Sam. 1:6–7). Depressed so that she could not eat, Hannah left the table. Alone and miserable with crying, she entered the temple and fell to her knees. With all his kindness, Elkanah could not fully enter into the grief of his wife, nor did he have the faith his wife had. Grief is lonely. Alone she brought her problems to the Lord in prayer.

Hannah had a unique sense of the Lord's presence. For her, heaven was not far from earth. She did not have to call aloud, but the cry of her bruised spirit and her overwhelming desire for a child reached His compassionate and understanding heart. The depths of her misery reached the depths of God's mercy. Does God hear prayer?

If radio's slim fingers can pluck a melody
From night and toss it o'er a continent or sea;
If the petalled white notes of a violin are blown across the
    mountains or the city's din,

If songs, like crimson roses, are called from the blue air—
Why should mortals wonder, if God hears prayer?

—Author Unknown

When Eli, the high priest, saw Hannah prostrate, her lips quivering with emotion, her face flushed with earnest entreaty, he came to the coarse conclusion that she was drunk. Perhaps silent prayer was unusual. More likely, he saw so much drunkenness and licentiousness around the temple on feast days that he did not recognize true piety. It appears that he was a poor minister and a worse father. When Eli accused Hannah of being drunken, she quickly said, "No, my lord, I am a woman of a sorrowful spirit" (1 Sam. 1:15). And after she confided in Eli, he gave her his blessing.

Prayer is speaking with God. Desire is the very soul of prayer. Hannah had taken the only right course. She had poured out her heart before God and had found a refuge in Him (Ps. 62). Hannah found power in prayer, comfort and peace. Her face shone with a new light because she had been in the presence of the Lord of Hosts. Hannah went back to Elkanah renewed and fortified in spirit. In the morning she worshiped with the family, and so she began both the day and the journey with God.

"Is any among you afflicted? let him pray" (James 5:13). Is any anxious? Let him, "by prayer and supplication with thanksgiving" (Phil. 4:6), make his requests known to God. This Hannah had done, again and again. The Lord answered her prayer and, before the next annual feast day, He gave her a son whom she called Samuel, *heard of God*.

Hannah's Praise

Hannah believed with all her heart that God was the Creator of children and that He alone could make her a mother. For years her most ardent prayers had been for a child. Now that the Lord had fulfilled her deepest desire, she recalled the vow she had made at Shiloh the year before. She had promised to give her son to the

Lord all the days of his life. The strength of her gentle and humble character is seen in the responsibility her husband gave her for this important decision concerning his son, Samuel (1 Sam. 1:23).

Hannah surrounded little Samuel with all the love and care that a devoted mother can give to her firstborn. She gratefully cared for her precious son whom she knew to be God's free gift. She never left him in the care of others, even declining a trip to Shiloh rather than leave him. She did not feel the need to get away from her family for a vacation.

When Samuel was weaned and somewhat able to care for himself (which may have been at the age of five or six—considering he was already able to help with little temple tasks), she dressed him for his first trip to Shiloh where she planned to leave him.

It must have been hard for her to part from him. She could have found many excuses for breaking her vow. There was the polluted atmosphere in the temple, the bad influence of Eli's sons (1 Sam. 2:22–24), and the inadequacies of old Eli. If Hannah had no fears for her son, it was because she placed him in the care and protection of God. She dedicated her son to the Order of the Nazarenes with a burnt offering, and to the Lord's service with a joyful, thankful heart.

Hannah was grateful that her son, young as he was, could perform little services in the tabernacle. He did them so well that Eli gave him a tiny ephod to wear. Each year when Hannah went up to Shiloh, she visited him and brought him a new coat, which she stitched herself, to wear with the white vest.

When Eli saw her unselfish attitude, he prayed that the Lord would bless her with other children. Imagine the happiness of Hannah when God gave her a family of five children to love and care for. We can be sure she taught them to pray and trust and praise.

Her song of praise is called the *Magnificat* of the Old Testament. In it Hannah expressed the depth, fervency, and joy of a happy woman who gives God all the glory, not only for giving her a son, but for what He is to all—a God of knowledge, justice, power, and salvation.

Have your children been asked of the Lord? How many of your children have been sincerely dedicated to God? Do you thank God for every happiness as Hannah did? Pray that the "Hannah-spirit" may characterize your life: "And I will wait upon the Lord . . . behold I and the children Thou hast given me . . . will serve the Lord with gladness."

Suggestions for Discussion

1. Is prayer a natural impulse, or is it an art—that is, something we must learn to do?
2. May we ask God for anything we want?
3. Sarah, Rachel, and Rebekah were barren, just as Hannah had been. How did each of these women react to her trial?
4. How often had the Lord commanded that the feast be kept? See Exodus 23:14–17. How often did Elkanah go? See Judges 21:19; and 1 Samuel 1:3; 2:19. What can we learn from Elkanah?
5. How did Eli err in his view of Hannah? What does that teach us? Notice that, though Eli had personal shortcomings, Hannah received his words with reverence and joy.
6. Do you think pastors should have more extensive training in the field of psychology, sociology, and counseling? Why? Why not?
7. Hannah dedicated her child to God. Do parents have the right to choose a profession (e.g., the ministry, medicine, and so on) for their children? Give reasons for your answer.
8. Describe Hannah's character. How can Hannah's story benefit us?
9. Compare Hannah's "Song of Triumph" (1 Sam. 2:1–10) and the *Magnificat* of Mary (Luke 1:46–55).

Fast ye for me . . . . : I also and my maidens will fast likewise; and so will I go in unto the king, . . . and if I perish, I perish.
—Esther 4:16

16

Esther

Scripture Reading
The Book of Esther

$\mathcal{T}$he book of Esther is the last historical book of the Old Testament and is logically placed with those of Ezra and Nehemiah because its history belongs to that period. The language of the book is Hebrew but it contains more Persian words than the books of Ezra and Nehemiah.

Ahasuerus was apparently dead when the story was written (Esther 10:2). The author was intimately acquainted with Persian court customs, had possible access to the chronicles of the court, and was a friend, certainly an admirer, of Mordecai. It was written, not for the Palestinian Jews, but for the Jews in Dispersion. It is a story that is very compact and complete, and is in some ways in a class by itself.

The book has no immediate connection with the other Bible books, and because it is so complete and dramatic, it has been called a legend, meant to depict the conditions of the Jews in the

Dispersion. And it does have all the elements of a myth or of a novel: it tells of the power of an ancient monarch, the beauty of the captive maiden who through unusual circumstances replaced royalty, of intrigue and murder, of lust and love, of revenge and the inevitable peaceful and happy ending.

Very noticeable is the omission of the name of God in any form in the book. This sets it apart from the other books of the Bible, for even the shortest psalm mentions the name of God. Neither is Jerusalem, the temple, or the law mentioned. Two historical facts are recorded, both of which relate to the captivity (Esther 2:6; 3:8).

However, the Jews have always accorded the book of Esther special honor and read it in their synagogues at every annual feast of Purim. When the names of Haman or of his family are read, the congregation vocally shows contempt for the man who, but for the grace of God, would have exterminated the Jews as a nation. To them, as well as to us, the book of Esther is the story of God's providential care of His people, of how He watches over them and will not allow His people to perish though they be scattered to the ends of the earth. They are His peculiar treasure, and though they may for a time forsake His ways, "Behold, he that keepeth Israel shall neither slumber nor sleep" (Ps. 121:4) but shall keep them and preserve them from this time forth and forevermore.

The King

There are five striking characters in this book that reads like a historical novel. They are Ahasuerus the king, Vashti the deposed queen, Esther the queen who succeeded Vashti, Haman the court favorite, and Mordecai the Jew. The first chapter tells us about the king, his princes, his queen, and the beautiful palace in which he gave a royal feast.

This Persian king, Ahasuerus, is distinguished from the Ahasuerus of Ezra 4:6 and the one of Daniel 9:1. This Ahasuerus is generally believed to be the king whom the Greeks called Xerxes, and what we read of him in Esther quite agrees with what we learn from secular history about him. He was the king who ruled over Persia when that immense empire reached its tentacles from Ethiopia to India. The Persian Empire was greater than any ancient empire had ever been before and can be compared in scope with England in her prime.

Ahasuerus stripped every subdued nation of its riches, using them chiefly to enhance his magnificence. He demanded exorbitant taxes and gifts of the conquered peoples that he might live in the splendor for which the Persian rulers were famous. It is believed that he was the Xerxes who led two million soldiers (more for display than service) against the Greeks and was defeated. He brought a tremendous fleet into the Mediterranean and, when he lost the naval battle, like a proud and furious god, demanded that his men chain the sea. He was haughty and pompous. What to him was a million men— the conquest must go on!

It was likely at this feast, of which we read in chapter one, that plans were made and supplies promised for the invasion of Greece. The feast was given in the third year of his reign when the affairs of the empire had quieted down sufficiently to allow the princes and nobles to leave their far-flung provinces for an extended visit in the capital, there to feast and celebrate with the king and to hear his plans for further conquest.

The great king showed his guests from one hundred twenty provinces—his satraps, princes, and many Median noblemen— regal hospitality unequaled anywhere. "He showed the riches of his glorious kingdom and the honor of his excellent majesty many days, even a hundred and fourscore days" (Esther 1:4). The feast was given in Shushan, his summer palace, renowned for its Oriental splendor. What king was as great as he who could build a special banqueting palace around the court of the garden large enough to entertain thousands? He laid it out lavishly with colored marble floors. On all sides bright hangings were fastened through huge silver rings on massive marble columns with cords of fine linen and rich purples from Tyre. With the plunder of the nations he had enough gold and silver beds or couches made for all his many guests. The excess of his magnificence is pointed out when we are told that each of the golden wine goblets was different from the others. And this proud sovereign would outdo even himself, for when the prolonged feast was over he made another for the men of Shushan.

From the colorful description of this feast we can picture the mighty monarch with heavy jeweled crown, in royal purple stitched in gold and stiff with jewels, as he reclines at a long, low cedar table. His princes are also lavishly dressed in royal colors and gem-studded sandals, and on dazzling couches near him they fawningly seek the despot's favor. The tables scintillate with gold and jewels, and odors of delicacies and royal wine mingle with the attar of roses and flowers for which the palace gardens are so famous. The seven days of feasting are ending with great hilarity, and the vain king, pleased with himself and "merry with wine," decides to climax the festivities by showing off his greatest treasure, his beautiful wife, Queen Vashti. The queen, who is entertaining the women at a royal feast, refuses to come at the king's command and he is furious. He has been disobeyed! Following the advice of his councilors, Vashti is deposed. So Vashti leaves the grandeur of the palace in obscurity, but not in shame, for in her refusal to be disgraced she shows dignity, nobility, and respect for the national custom that does not allow its women to appear unveiled in the presence of men, least of all, drunken, reveling men. So Vashti, shining like a meteor for a moment, fades from view.

The Queen

Perhaps two years after this, Ahasuerus, having come back from his exploit against Greece defeated and dejected, turned to the pleasures of the *seraglio* (the harem). Tiring of his concubines he remembered Vashti. He loved Vashti (though himself and honor more) and had been inordinately proud of her. His thinking of her now with regret cast a gloom over the entire court. His high officers and eunuchs, to cheer the king, suggested that it was time to choose a new queen. The greatest beauty in the empire would be his for the choosing, for they would arrange a beauty contest. The king agreed, and soon fair maidens from every part of the empire were brought to Shushan and taken into the house of the virgins by eunuchs who provided each one with oils and perfumes for their purification (Esther 2:9, 12), seven maiden attendants, and any apparel they might desire to wear for the evening that each girl went into the king's royal apartment. The one with whom the king was the most pleased would be crowned with Vashti's crown. In the months that followed, young women of every kind and color, from the dusky beauties of Ethiopia and India, to proud princesses of ruined kingdoms—some aspiring, some fearful—spent a night with the sated sovereign and were in the morning assigned to the house of the women where they remained as the king's concubines (Esther 2:14).

Now, there was a Jew of the tribe of Benjamin named Mordecai living in Shushan who served either as a porter at the king's gate (Esther 2:21) or as a eunuch, considering that he was admitted into the court of the women's house every day (Esther 2:11). Years before he had adopted, or taken into his home and heart, his young orphaned cousin, Hadassah. Her Persian name was Esther (meaning star, after the goddess Ishtar). She was obedient and intelligent and grew up to be superbly beautiful. Mordecai, who saw and heard everything that went on at the king's gate, was sure that no one as fair as Esther had been admitted. Gambling on good fortune for his adopted daughter, and hoping to attain prestige for himself and favors for his captive people, Mordecai one day offered Esther as a candidate for royal favor—a sacrifice to the royal slave of passion.

There is some question as to Esther's willingness, which is inferred from her lack of interest in special adornment (Esther 2:15). Although a Persian Jew might well have considered the king's favor a high honor, Esther may have gone only out of obedience to Mordecai (Esther 2:10). From subsequent events we see that Esther was a dutiful girl who remained deeply loyal to her foster father.

When Esther was taken into the women's house, the chamberlain was so favorably impressed with Esther that he gave her special favors. When her turn came to go into the king, everyone who saw her was arrested by her loveliness. She must have been exquisitely beautiful, her mien outstanding and different from the other virgins, to so captivate the connoisseur of charm, the great Ahasuerus. Was it only physical beauty that caused the king to choose Esther from among all the gorgeous girls? He must have seen intelligence, integrity, and courage in Esther—not a fawning but a queenly character. With great pride and ceremony Ahasuerus placed the royal crown on Esther's shining curls and made her queen of all Persia (Esther 2:17). He "made a great feast, unto all his princes and his servants, even Esther's feast" (Esther 2:18) and gave gifts to all the provinces.

God's Overruling Providence

For five years all went well (Esther 2:16; 3:7). Esther lived in luxury; she was honored and adored by all. Though far above Mordecai in station, Esther did not forget him. In all these years she had respected his command to keep her racial identity a secret. Mordecai was still to her a beloved foster father and benefactor, and she kept in constant touch with him through her chamberlain, Hatach, and her maids.

Haman, the Agagite of Amalekite descent (perhaps from the royal family of that Arabian tribe), had risen to highest favor in the Persian court. The king and Haman were constantly together. The king was so infatuated with his favorite that he commanded, with no obvious reason, ostentatious reverence for him. The hate of the Amalekite for the Jew had survived the centuries, and when Mordecai the Jew refused to bow before him, Haman was beside himself with anger.

Queen Esther found out how great Haman's power and hate had become when Hatach reported that Mordecai was seen in the city, and even at the king's gates, in great distress, though signs of mourning were prohibited in the royal area. When ascertaining the cause, Esther first heard of the horrible massacre planned for her entire race. The perpetrator was known to be the wicked Haman, whose hate for Mordecai had become such a consuming passion that he had bribed the king with the tempting sum of two million dollars for the privilege of killing *all* the Jews (Esther 3:2–15), and then had appealed to the lust of his countrymen to have the deed accomplished.

When the queen read a copy of the decree, which Hatach had brought from Mordecai, she was greatly grieved. The decree constituted the virtual annihilation of her people, for all of Palestine was also in the Persian Empire. Messages were quickly, and in secret, carried between Esther and Mordecai by faithful Hatach. Mordecai told the queen to use her influence with Ahasuerus to save her people, but Esther knew well the penalty for going to see the king unbidden and was afraid. Capricious and absolute, his frown meant death. Only Haman and the seven princes were allowed that privilege. Fear clutched at her heart—perhaps she was already out of favor. Was it Haman who had kept her from her husband these many days? Then certain death awaited her!

While Esther hesitated, Mordecai became the more disturbed and his appeal could not be set aside. When he insisted, "Who knoweth whether thou art come to the kingdom for such a time as this?" (Esther 4:14)—a challenge to every Christian since—Esther knew that she must try to save her people. Though elevation to a high position is a test of character, Esther had not forgotten her father's God, nor lost her love for her people, nor her moral courage. We see faith and trust in God in her request that the Jews of Shushan fast. The fast included a cry or prayer (Esther 4:16; 9:31). Her own fasting is indicative of her religious convictions and of habitual devotions. With sincerity, earnestness, and courage buoyed up by faith in the power and providence of God, Esther sent the word: "I go in unto the king, which is not according to the law: and if I perish, I perish" (Esther 4:16).

Laying aside her garments of sackcloth at the end of the three days fast, Esther dressed in royal apparel. Pale but composed after her fasting and prayer, she came to the king "all glorious within: her clothing is of wrought gold . . . in raiment of needlework: the virgins her companions follow her . . . into the king's palace" (Ps. 45:13–15). Facing the gate from his elevated throne in the pillared hail, the king was astonished to see Esther coming, regally and reverently, into the court. What a moment of suspense. What immeasurable relief when the king held out his golden scepter! Had he been once again dazzled by her beauty? He did not know that "the king's heart is in the hand of the LORD, as the rivers of water: he turneth it whithersoever he will" (Prov. 21:1).

Did Ahasuerus sense that a real need had occasioned Esther's visit, or was it royal magnanimity that made him say, "What wilt thou . . . what is thy request? it shall be even given thee to the half of the kingdom" (Esther 5:3). With tact and prudence Esther replied by inviting both the king and Haman to a banquet in her house, where she might present her request in more favorable circumstances. At the banquet the next day the king again said, "What is thy petition? . . . It shall be performed" (Esther 5:6). Esther waited until the following day, when she prepared a similar banquet, to plead for her own life and for that of her people. When she pointed to Haman, the would-be murderer, the king was aghast. Furiously he strode into the palace garden. When he returned to the dining hall, he found Haman cringing on Esther's couch and instantly condemned the wicked prince to be hanged on the gallows that Haman had himself erected the evening before for Mordecai, the Jew.

Soon another decree went forth to all the realm of Persia. This gave the Jews the right to defend themselves on the thirteenth day of the twelfth month, which is the month of Adar, for which day Haman had cast the lot, or *Pur*, for their destruction. The decree was written by Mordecai the Jew and bore the authority of the king's seal. And Mordecai went out from the king's presence in royal apparel. Mordecai was great and wise, "seeking the wealth of his people, and speaking peace to all his seed" (Esther 10:3). And the Jews everywhere had light and gladness and joy and honor.

God moves in a mysterious way
His wonders to perform:
He plants His footsteps in the sea,
And rides upon the storm.

Deep in unfathomable mines
Of never failing skill,
He treasures up His bright designs,
And works His sovereign will.

Ye fearful saints, fresh courage take;
The clouds ye so much dread
Are big with mercy, and shall break
In blessings on your head.
—William Cowper

Suggestions for Discussion

1. What do you think of the decree of Ahasuerus—that every man should have the rule in his own house (Esther 1:22)? Was this edict in his domain? Is it a popular idea today? Is it scriptural?
2. When Esther was taken to the king, she required no special gowns or ornaments (Esther 2:15). What does this indicate?
3. Esther obtained the favor of all who looked upon her. How can we obtain the favor and good will of others?
4. Did Esther do right or wrong in concealing her identity?
5. What good characteristics does Esther appear to have had?
6. Many say that Esther was a wicked woman: she was wrong to leave her good home for a heathen one, she committed adultery by marrying the king, and she requested an extra day for revenge for her people (Esther 9:12–16). What is your opinion of this appraisal of Esther?

7. The Feast of Purim was made an annual affair (Esther 9:20–22). Is it good to remember past sorrows and trials, or is it better to relegate all such things to the past? Why?

8. What would you say is the most important lesson taught by the book of Esther? Name some others as well.

9. Show how God's providence is seen throughout the story.

Behold the handmaid of the Lord; be it unto me according to thy word.
—Luke 1:38

17

Mary

The Mother of the Great Son

Scripture Reading
Matthew 1:16–25; 2; 12:46–50; 13:55–58;
Luke 1:26–56; 2; John 19:25–27; Acts 1:14

𝒜mong all the women of sacred history, Mary is unique. She is unique not because she is holy (free from sin and its consequences, as a segment of Christendom teaches) but because she is the mother of the Great Son. There is only one Jesus, and there can only be one mother of Jesus. As a mother, she is one of us, but, as the mother of the Great Son, she is preeminent.

Mary was one of us—often anxious, troubled, pained, tired, and sad. She drank deeply of most exquisite joy, but also tasted as great sorrow as a life can hold. Her son was a man of sorrows, well acquainted with grief. Men hid, as it were, their faces from Him, and Mary witnessed it all. Being in every sense a loyal and loving mother a "sword pierced her own heart also." Her son was misunderstood and mocked. Mary, too, was misunderstood. She also knew the frustration of not understanding her own son. But there is never a hint of self-pity, not a word of complaint from Mary. She, who received a rich measure of the grace of God, kept all these things to herself, pondering them in her heart.

Christian art has caught the spirit of Mary and has touchingly portrayed her as the Mother of Sorrows, pensive and sad—sweet and trustingly yielding her mind, soul, and body to the will of God. All the world has since Mary's day echoed, as a melodious refrain, the words of the angel: "Blessed art thou among women" (Luke 1:28), for adoration of Mary is timeless, raceless, classless, and ageless. Every people and nation has conceived of Mary and the Christ child as being one of them. The Italian represents Mary and her child as southern Europeans; the African paints Jesus a dark-skinned infant; in the East, Mary and Jesus are Asians; and the American artist, Melchers, like the famous Dutch painters, has depicted Mary as a Hollander. With a feeling of kinship and reverent joy, people everywhere will always confess, with Elisabeth the mother of John the Baptist, "[Thou art] the mother of my Lord" (Luke 1:43).

Mary the Maiden

Nazareth was a small, little-known village in lower Galilee. Its limestone and clay-walled houses were built on the declivity of a hill. A valley spread out before it with mountains all around. To the west was Mount Carmel hallowed with memories of venerable Elijah; to the east and south the heights of Tabor and bleak Gilboa were plainly visible. From Mary's hillside town she could look out upon the plain of Esdraelon and recall from among ancient tales the story of Deborah, whose song she knew. And beyond the blood-drenched valley of the centuries were the blue mountains of Samaria. But Nazareth with its gardens, groves of date palms, fig trees, pomegranates, and fields of wheat and barley was an insignificant village and proverbially of little account. "Can there any good thing come out of Nazareth?" (John 1:46). "Come and see," said Philip. Nazareth is not mentioned in history or named in the Old Testament, yet the Son of Promise was designated as Jesus of Nazareth.

Here, in a modest home, a young Jewish woman by the name of Mary (or Miriam in the Hebrew) lived with her father. The daughter of Heli, she was of the tribe of Judah, as was Joseph, though descended from a different family. Most interpreters say that Matthew's genealogy is that of Joseph and Luke's that of Mary. Genealogy was highly important to the Hebrews, and both Matthew and Luke recount the generations to prove to the Jews that Jesus was the Christ, the promised Messiah.

Mary lived in the fullness of time. For long years her people had waited with earnest expectation for Israel's Deliverer. In Mary's day the Jewish people were caught between two millstones: the Roman government that pressed yokelike upon farmers and artisan alike, and the scribes and doctors of the law who enforced their ritual and law to the letter, demanding the tithe even from the hungry. There was more fear of the law of the Rabbis than true worship of God in Galilee. There were many strangers within the gates who had no fear of God at all. It was a time of oppression and sin. Even the Holy City and the sacred temple were corrupt. The darkness, weariness, and sorrow of the world were awaiting the tread of Messiah's footsteps.

When we first meet Mary she is engaged to Joseph, the carpenter of Nazareth. Joseph, devout and kind, was thought to be considerably older than Mary who was, perhaps, eighteen or twenty years old at this time. After appropriate formalities of presenting the coin from the groom to the bride, the dowry stipulated, the signing of the betrothal papers (as binding as marriage), and choosing the two groomsmen—one for the bride and one for the groom—the betrothal of the happy pair was celebrated by feasting with friends and relatives. After this a period of waiting ensued.

Joseph had chosen well, for though Mary was poor she was of royal blood. Scripture does not describe her appearance, but she must have been lovely to look at. Mary has been beautifully represented by many artists, but we must remember that she was Jewish and that her features were characteristic of her race. We can most accurately picture her with black hair, a broad forehead, lustrous dark eyes with long lashes, and a rich, deep complexion. There was kindness in her heart and sweet charm in her smile, which won the noble heart of Joseph.

Mary and Gabriel

We can assume that Mary was more serious and pious than most girls in Nazareth and was often found in the place of prayer. Every devout parent provided such a place. There the Torah, or Scripture rolls, and family records were kept. Usually a corner of the roof or an inner chamber was reserved for the place of meditation and prayer. Mary believed in the power of God and, no doubt, often read the books of Esther and Ruth, and was familiar with the prophecies concerning the Messiah. As Sarah, David, and Hannah before her, Mary awaited the Messiah with inexpressible longing. It may well be, as Titian has painted her, that she was in the prayer room pondering the prophecy of Isaiah when she was startled by the heavenly visitor who suddenly stood before her, luminous with eternal youth, beauty, and glory. Thousands of years before, this same Gabriel had brought the promise of a Redeemer to Abraham and had, some hundreds of years later, told Daniel when the Messiah could be expected (Dan. 9:20–27). The silence of the years was broken once again when Gabriel came to one highly favored out of all womankind—demure, quiet, and humble Mary in her parental home in obscure Nazareth.

The angel came with an astonishing salutation: "Hail, thou that art highly favored, the Lord is with thee: blessed art thou among women" (Luke 1:28). The quiet of the prayer room was shattered by celestial brilliance and electrified by the other-world voice of Gabriel. Though startled, Mary did not cry out in terror but quietly pondered what this could mean. The angel had come vested with a divine commission—and how stupendous was his message: "Thou shalt conceive in thy womb, and bring forth a son . . . JESUS . . . the

Son of the Highest" (Luke 1:31–32). We see only firm faith in her response to the angel in her first words, "How shall this be, seeing I know not a man?" (Luke 1:34). The angel answered that the body of Jesus would be created by an act of divine power (Luke 1:35). Though Mary was troubled about the implications of such an unusual event, with a faith and resignation that will never be surpassed, she said, "Behold the handmaid of the Lord; be it unto me according to thy word" (Luke 1:38). Such complete resignation and surrender of the heart to God makes Mary, by God's grace, a truly noble woman. With the visit of the angel to Mary, the most divine and merciful idea ever conceived in eternity was actualized, bringing the era of light, peace, and good will to men of all peoples forever. The shining angel soared heavenward and Mary was left alone to ponder and to pray, to thrill with inexpressible joy, and to praise with deep humility. No doubt she recalled the promise made to her people, "Behold, a virgin shall conceive, and bear a son, and shall call his name Immanuel" (Isa. 7:14). What emotions awoke in her young soul—what ecstasy to be chosen the mother of the Messiah, the King whose dominion is universal and everlasting!

Mary must leave her room and meet her family and her friends with this great and almost unbelievable secret in her heart. For who would believe such a story as hers? An angel had not been seen on earth by anyone for over four hundred years. Surely an angel might visit the great Abraham, but she was only an unknown village maiden who watered the flocks and filled the pitcher each evening at the village well. Her closest friends, perhaps even her mother and father, would have thought her delirious—her story preposterous—if she had told it. The scribes would have sagely said, "Out of Galilee ariseth no prophet!" What of her royal lineage—but of what value was it, her friends would query. Many generations had passed since David's line had been of any influence. She dared not tell Joseph. How could he believe her story? And what would he say or think of her? Yet with God nothing is impossible—had not the angel said so? As long as she lived she would never forget Gabriel. The angel's every word was indelibly impressed on her memory. She cherished his words in her heart, and it is possible many years later she recounted them to Luke the evangelist.

The Trip to Hebron

Mary remembered that the angel had said cousin Elisabeth was also going to have a child in her old age, like Sarah of old. (It may be that Mary had no mother at this time with whom she could share her mighty secret and that she hesitated to confide in her sister Salome.) She would go to Elisabeth—*she* would understand! For this long journey of some hundred miles she would need provisions. She made haste to go. Quickly she walked the steep path from her hilltop home to the plain—traveling alone or with those she met on the way to the town of the priests where Elisabeth and her husband lived. The well-worn path she traveled was southward through country rich with the history of God's people. Who knew the tumult of her thoughts—still amazed, sometimes perplexed, then joyous—as again and again she recalled the words of the prophets who had walked this very plain, saying "Behold Messiah cometh." Her heart throbbed with deep emotion as she approached the holy city and then, beyond pleasant little Bethlehem, she came to Hebron. Did her wonderful secret shine in her eyes and make her pretty face at once animated and tranquil? Were those who spoke to her on the road or walked a little way with her somehow warmed and inspired by the lovely girl who lived under the shadow of the Almighty?

The last dusty mile of the trek finally brought her to Elisabeth's door where she was warmly welcomed. Before Mary could lay aside her veil or rest her tired feet, this saintly woman filled with the Holy Spirit exclaimed, "Blessed art thou among women. . . . and whence is this to me, that the mother of my Lord should come to me?" (Luke 1:42–43). At the words of Elisabeth, Mary's fears fled. She was happy, her brightest hopes were confirmed and her faith was strengthened. Her pent up emotions were released, and love, joy, hope, humility, and praise cascaded into a rapturous song that we call the *Magnificat*—a beautiful song of praise (Luke 1:46–55). What a blessed time these two women had, having both been chosen by God for such great things, as they visited for three happy months.

Mary and Joseph

Just before the birth of Elisabeth's child, Mary returned to her home in Nazareth, for the time was near that Joseph would take her into his house. Both Mary and Joseph had looked forward to the coming nuptials. Here Mary, still at her parental home, met her first trial. Village gossip was inevitable in this little town. Did it reach the ears of Joseph that Mary, his betrothed virgin, was with child? What a choice morsel for gossip—Mary, young and pure as she was lovely, had been untrue to the grave, honest carpenter who loved her with the mature affections of a man with the experiences of life behind him. Mary whispered the truth to Joseph, but the story she told was so incredulous! He loved her and trusted her, but this story seemed impossible! Joseph could not believe it. His suspicions were natural, excusable, but how Joseph's doubts and the wagging tongues and averted looks of the villagers must have hurt Mary!

After much thought and prayer, the shocked and deeply hurt Joseph decided to divorce Mary. The Jewish penalty for infidelity was severe (Lev. 20:10). But Joseph was a just and kindly man, and, rather than make a public spectacle of the girl he loved, he chose to give her a private divorce (Matt. 1:19), which he could do without publicly specifying the cause. Weary with strain and disappointment, he bowed his head on his arm on the sawdust of his work bench and fell asleep. Artists have chosen to portray Joseph thus when the angel appeared to him in a dream and told him to take Mary as his wife. Joseph's fears were calmed, his doubts dispelled; he was happy once more in Mary's love. And to the lasting credit of the humble carpenter of Nazareth, the Scripture says that he "did as the angel of the Lord had bidden him, and took unto him his wife" (Matt. 1:24). It must have been a strange and awesome thing to learn that his beloved Mary was to be the mother of the Messiah and that he, out of all men, had been chosen to be the foster father to watch over the infant son of the Most High God.

Mary's Child Jesus

Even though we find only a glimpse of Mary here and there on the sacred pages, hers is the most sublime story ever told. The tale of her trip to Bethlehem, and of the birth of the Savior on a truss of hay in a cattle cave, is world renowned.

It was a holy night when Jesus the Savior was born. The sky was filled with a myriad of heavenly beings who announced to all the world, "Glory to God in the highest, and on earth peace, good will toward men" (Luke 2:14). The before-dawn visit of the shepherds—their clothes wet with dew of the Judean hillsides, their rough faces alight with the glory they had seen—brought a story strange and awesome. Mary had much food for thought and need for pondering, and both reason for happiness and need for strong faith.

In Bethlehem, on the eighth day and according to Jewish law (Gen. 17:12), Mary's child was circumcised and named *Jesus*. Often it was neighbors or relatives, happy with the new parents, who gave the child a name (e.g., Ruth 4:17). The precious name of Jesus, hope of earth and joy of heaven, was brought to Mary by the great Gabriel, personal messenger of the Almighty. Little did Mary comprehend what it would cost her son, in love and agony, to bear the name above every name.

The new mother's days passed rapidly, and the baby was nearly six weeks old when, obeying Jewish law for her purification, Mary went to Jerusalem. How exciting it was to be in the temple with her special child! In the court of the women she met other mothers with their babies and offerings. Mary was poor and had little to bring—just two doves, which the priest took from her after perhaps reading aloud from Leviticus twelve. It is not dishonorable to be poor—far better to be rich toward God! Even Jesus the God-man had no place that He could call His own. More blessed are the poor in spirit who are washed in the blood of the Lamb than those sprinkled to purification by the blood of doves and pigeons.

Now followed the presentation of Jesus, the firstborn who had to be redeemed because all firstborn and firstfruits belonged to God (Exod. 13:2; 34:20). Hardly had this holy act been completed when, to Mary's amazement, the withered old figure who had come shuffling along the pillared archway into the court of the women stood before her. Priest and onlookers alike were dumbfounded, for well-known and devout Simeon, his beard white as the snow of winter, saw in this tiny baby the salvation of Israel. Filled with the Holy Spirit, aged Simeon took the baby in his arms and praised God with a loud voice, blessing Mary and her child.

Almost at the same time, the bent figure of old Anna the prophetess emerged from the shadows. She, too, saw the light of God in the face of the child. Reverently beholding the baby in Simeon's arms, she confirmed his prophetic words. How Mary marveled at the solemn but glorious predictions of Simeon and Anna, coming so soon after the amazing testimony of the shepherds.

No less astounding was the visit of the wise men who had followed the star to her house in Bethlehem. Breathlessly, she watched as they worshiped her son. What princely gifts those foreigners brought this child of the swaddling clothes! Mary had never seen such wealth before!

The Flight into Egypt

How soon the powers of evil changed joy into fear. After the visit of the wise men, Joseph was warned in a dream to take the young child and his mother and flee to Egypt. Everyone knew of the horrible cruelty of depraved Herod, and Joseph lost no time. He hurriedly packed his few tools, the wise men's gifts, clothing, and provisions into the donkey's saddlebags. After helping Mary and her baby to mount the donkey, they left Bethlehem.

Hastened on by serious peril, the little family likely took the shortest route to Egypt—down the barren Judean hills, onto the plains of Philistia, and from there to the coast and Gaza the last of the cities. Then over the brilliant, hot, desert sands, blown about into drifts and dotted by cropping limestone. The desert sun was fierce, beating down on the head of Mary, her back weary with the burden of the growing child tucked into the long scarf that draped from her head and was secured at her side. The silence of the wastelands was broken only by the slow clop, clop of the donkey on the hard-baked coastal plain and the occasional quiet talk of Joseph comforting Mary, who was going through a fearful and trying experience.

A donkey cannot travel fast. It meant prodding the little animal along for at least two weeks to cover the two hundred fifty miles from Bethlehem to the new home in Egypt. Exhausted, Mary reached the land of Israel's bondage. Wearily she rested in the shade of the palms and, crossing the river, the little family likely reached Alexandria where they found a large Jewish settlement and safety. Some claim that they stayed in Mataria near Cairo in a cave home shown today to tourists.

Jesus spent the first years of his life in Egypt. Here, in a pagan town, amid worshipers of Re and Isis, among a people who hated her race, Mary first prayed with her son. Here Mary sang to her son "The Lord Our God Is One God" and all the songs of Zion she knew. Did Mary and Joseph search the Scriptures and in it read: "Out of Egypt I have called my son"? You can be sure that both constantly sought Palestinian travelers for news from home.

Once again an angel came with the good news that it was safe to return home (Matt. 2:20). With implicit faith, Joseph again hurried to obey and trekked—gladly, this time—the gray and yellow desert beyond which was home. They did not return to Bethlehem, however, because Joseph heard that Archelaus (who succeeded Herod the Great) was as cruel as his father before him, and so he "turned aside into . . . Galilee" (Matt. 2:22). After these years, which were unsettled and lonely, Mary and Joseph were happy to be back home in Nazareth. Jesus was a little boy now, and the villagers saw, for the first time, the child who was conceived of the Holy Spirit and born of the Virgin Mary. Then followed long uneventful years in Mary's hometown. No angel came to visit; it seems that nothing spectacular happened at all.

Mary the Mother

The trials of Mary matured her early. She was a conscientious mother, one who felt the presence and power of the living God, one who could speak of His mercies and who had faith in His promises. Mother Mary watched over her son through His formative years with loving care, gently cherishing, feeding, and clothing Him. Daily she read the Scriptures to Him and taught Him, most likely sending Him to the rabbi school, and He grew in wisdom and favor with God and man (Luke 2:52). She took Him to worship in the synagogue and on annual trips to Jerusalem for the feast. Here His consciousness of eternal purpose was increased.

Mary's alone was the privilege of rearing a perfect child, One in whom was no sin or guile. The boy Jesus heard God in everything around Him and saw His beauty everywhere. This was *His Father's* world. Mary's child had perfect, uninterrupted fellowship with the Father, and gradually developed to the full consciousness of His mission. Jesus, like any other Jewish lad, was soon helping His father in the shop, shaping yokes and mending plows and buckets. After Joseph died, it is presumed that Jesus took over His father's business, becoming the carpenter of Nazareth (Mark 6:3). If ever there was heaven on earth, it was in that Galilean home of poverty and toil. What power of prayer, what hallowed fellowship between father, mother, and the God-son within those lowly walls. Home is still a sacred place when Jesus is there.

When Jesus was twelve years of age His parents took Him to Jerusalem for the Passover. When Jewish boys were twelve they were first permitted to take an active part in the temple offering. After seven crowded feast days in the Holy City, Mary and Joseph with friends and relatives—perhaps Mary's sister and her family—

joined the throngs of pilgrims on the dusty road toward home. The roads leading to Jerusalem were always crowded with caravans, traders and their freighted camels, donkeys with bulging burdens, and people walking—especially during the feast days. At the end of the day Mary found, to her dismay, that Jesus was not with them. It was a very human mother—distressed, worried, upset—that impulsively said, "Why, son . . . ," when at last she found Him. "Wist ye not . . . ," was His reply. She knew better than anyone else that the angel of the Lord would watch over Him and that He had come to do His Father's will. "Wist ye not that I must be about my Father's business?" (Luke 2:49). They knew it—without *actually* knowing or understanding. To Mary this was the first real inkling of coming separation, and Mary pondered this, too, in her heart.

After the visit to Jerusalem, Jesus spent eighteen years, called the hidden years, at home with his mother. It is conjectured that Joseph passed away and that Jesus, the eldest son, became His mother's support. Living such a normal, quiet life after such an auspicious beginning must have been a source of concern to Mary. Often, as one uneventful year followed another, she pondered the message of Gabriel, the words of Simeon, of the prophetess, of her inspired cousin. She thought of the shepherds and the night the angels shone like stars and the stars sang like angels. She was perplexed. Was the role of Jesus merely that of an exemplary son? Were great things still awaiting? Moreover, when Jesus finally began His ministry, He was baptized in the Jordan by John, whose teaching the venerable rabbis questioned.

The Mother of the Great Son

Mary must have heard about the voice that spoke from heaven saying, "This is my beloved Son, in whom I am well pleased" (Matt. 3:17). This new assurance of His divine Sonship may account for Mary's absolute confidence in His power at the wedding in Cana when she said, "They have no wine." It must have been a trying test of her faith when, in the presence of relatives and friends, her son called her not *mother*, but *woman* (John 2:3–4).

Mary followed the ministry of Jesus with pride, no doubt, but also with growing anxiety and with concern over His health because of His exhausting days with the multitudes that never left Him alone. She feared for His safety because of the bitter hatred of those who were envious, who despised Him, and who sought His life. It was Mary's mother-love and concern that prompted her to follow Jesus to Capernaum (Mark 3:31–35). Was she hurt or did she understand when, once again, the Great Son dismissed His personal relationship to His mother?

The sacrifice required of Mary at Capernaum was later demanded of her in the highest degree at Calvary. Hate apparently triumphed, and her precious and beloved son hung on the cross, nail pierced, covered with welts and torn flesh, His head bowed and bloody. She was with Him to the end. Her anguish, as she knelt in the shadow of the cross, was severe. Every mocking word, every evidence of pain, pierced her sensitive heart like the spear that was plunged into the side of her son. She was mute with sorrow. As the last human tie was breaking she was near Him. The Savior saw her there and, in His hour of deepest agony, remembered her love and devotion. He gave His precious mother into the care of His beloved disciple when He said, "Woman, behold thy son," and to John, "Behold thy mother" (John 19:26–27). Mary, the mother who gave the Son of Man life, became a woman for whom Christ died that she might evermore be with Him in glory.

The last time we see Mary is after the Resurrection in the Upper Room in Jerusalem. The disciples had come directly there after witnessing the Ascension on Mount Olivet. "These all continued with one accord in prayer and supplication, with the women, and Mary the mother of Jesus, and with his brethren" (Acts 1:14). The last place we see Mary, the mother of the Great Son, is in the seclusion of the Upper Room in the attitude of prayer. When we shall know as we are known, we shall meet Mary again in the temple not made with hands, eternal in the heavens. And her soul will magnify the Lord, and her spirit will rejoice in God her Savior, for the Lord God Almighty and the Lamb are the temple of the Celestial City (Rev. 21:22).

Suggestions for Discussion

1. Why do people disbelieve the story of the Virgin Birth? Which was the greater miracle, the Virgin Birth or God becoming man?
2. Discuss Mariolatry.
3. What do we learn about Mary's character during the visit with the angel (Luke 1:29, 34, 38)?
4. Read Mary's song (Luke 1:46–55). What does it reveal about her?
5. What qualifications did Joseph possess to be the foster father of Jesus?
6. It is generally believed that Mary and Joseph lived in Bethlehem for a time (Matt. 2:11). How do you suppose Joseph supported his family? What reason can you suggest for their prolonged stay in Bethlehem?
7. Who were among the first New Testament people to confess their faith in Jesus?
8. Try to imagine Mary's son as He played, studied, and worked; imagine His attitude toward His playmates, His parents, the natural world. Was He different from other children? Could Mary have had any problems with her child?
9. Do mothers today always understand their children? Give examples.
10. Did Mary have other children? Some say no, others yes. What do you think (e.g., Matt. 12:46–50; Mark 6:3; Acts 1:14)? If she did, why did Jesus tell John to take care of her?
11. What did Jesus teach us when He called Mary *woman* instead of *mother*?
12. What makes Mary great?

For with God nothing shall be impossible.
—Luke 1:37

18

Elisabeth

Scripture Reading
Luke 1

Luke, the gospel writer, could not speak as an eyewitness of the things that had happened concerning Jesus. He was not a companion of Jesus but was one of those who surely believed in Him, in His power, and the effectiveness of His ministry.

A beloved physician, Luke was a Gentile by birth, but he knew the God of Israel, knew the famous hymns sung by God's people, and believed the Old Testament prophecies (Luke 3:4–5). He knew that salvation was of the Jews but also believed that "all flesh shall see the salvation of God" (Luke 3:6).

He had heard all about the birth of Jesus and had read various accounts of His work. Luke interviewed those who were personal acquaintances of our Lord and talked with witnesses of all that had been done. From Acts, which Luke also wrote, we learn that he was a close friend of Paul, being his companion on missionary journeys, and went through many experiences with Paul (e.g., Acts 27; 28:2; Col. 4:14). Luke also knew Mark, the gospel writer, well (Col. 4:10, 14; 2 Tim. 4:11). He had listened to Paul preach and was convinced that Jesus was the Christ, the Son of God.

In his gospel narrative, Luke writes a full account including all the important facts in the history of our Lord. Luke is the only gospel writer who includes the political situation in which the principals of his story lived. He gives an accurate record of those who ruled in both the national and ecclesiastical spheres. It is important to know, not alone that Herod the Great ruled when Jesus was born, but that Caesar Augustus was emperor over all known provinces. When John the Baptist began his ministry, Luke again tells us who dominated the world and local scene (Luke 3:1–2). Luke wants all to know that Jesus was a world figure and that John's coming was of epoch-making importance. Luke was right. Even men today who do not believe the gospel date every letter they write from the time of the coming of our Lord.

The most sublime and world-renowned tale ever told is that of Luke, and it begins with the story of John the Baptist, the son of Elisabeth.

Elisabeth's Husband

Four hundred years had passed since Malachi had cried out, "Behold, I will send you Elijah the prophet before the coming of the great and dreadful day of the LORD" (Mal. 4:5).

The years were dark and long before the dawn of the Sun of Righteousness. We know from secular history that the Jews were dominated in turn by Persia (on whose throne Esther had sat); by Alexander the Great, world conqueror; by Egypt; then by the Syrian Antiochus Epiphanes, a cruel oppressor. During the hundred-year rule of the Maccabees there was some relief, but they were replaced by Rome and the Herods, who were some of the most godless, bloodthirsty men who ever lived. Herod the Great, who had ordered all babes in Bethlehem to be slain, married the last of the Maccabees, beautiful Marianne, whom he later killed in a fit of anger. Zacharias and Elisabeth knew many people who had suffered at the hand of this Herod.

These oppressive years were rife with fear and hate. Morality decayed, and there was corruption in both church and state. The priesthood was largely controlled by, and was at the mercy of, the Roman rulers.

The Jewish spiritual rulers were blind leaders of the blind. They rejected the Lamb of God, in whom all their sacrificial rites found fulfillment. They were corrupt and evil and involved politically (Matt. 26:3–5; John 19:12). Though there was only one high priest, Caiaphas, Annas also held a high position of great influence with likely political connections.

The darker the night of sin, the brighter shines the light of faith. Among the priests was at least one godly man—Zacharias of the course of Abia. This was the eighth class of the twenty-four groups in the priesthood once appointed by David (1 Chron. 24), each group having to serve for a week, the task of each priest to be determined by lot.

The priest Zacharias and his wife, Elisabeth, lived in Hebron, in the hill country of Ephraim. Hebron was the most ancient of cities. Here Abraham had lived (Gen. 13:18) and here, in the Cave of Macpelah, he lay buried with Sarah, his wife, Isaac and Rebecca, Jacob and Leah (Gen. 23:17–20). David once had his royal residence there (2 Sam. 2:3). Hebron, within walking distance of the temple at Jerusalem, was now the city of the priests.

When the course of Abia served their week, Zacharias was chosen to burn the incense in the Holy Place. It must have been a high day, or Sabbath, for the whole congregation was assembled in the outer court. Perhaps Elisabeth, surely pious Simeon and Anna the prophetess, were among those who awaited the blessing of the venerable priest.

Holding the sweet incense in his hand, Zacharias, whose heart was right with God and whose life was blameless before Him, stepped solemnly to the golden altar. As the burning incense distilled upward, the place was suddenly filled with crystal light scintillating from the golden altar and the golden shewbread table. It took a moment to see in the burst of shocking, blinding light the form of an angel. His awful glory struck fear in the heart of Zacharias, as it had to others before who had met the heavenly visitor. But when the voice from the brilliance said, "Fear not . . . thy prayer is heard; thy wife Elisabeth shall bear thee a son" (Luke 1:13), the good priest doubted. He and his wife had prayed and prayed so many years for a child, but now they were old people. They had accepted their lot—such a precious blessing was not for them. And now the angel promised a son to the aged priest, a son who would be a great man, filled with the Holy Spirit!

It was too good to be true—too hard to believe! "How shall I know?" he asked. "I am Gabriel," answered the angel. That was proof enough but, because Zacharias had not believed at once, his power of speech was taken away for a time. The angel went back to stand in God's presence. The gray-haired priest, his face mystified and radiant, went into the outer court where the people waited. He could not speak the blessing, but he carried in his heart the promise of joy, gladness, and blessing that would be to all people.

Elisabeth

How eagerly Elisabeth awaited her beloved husband at the end of his week of temple service. The twenty-mile walk seemed short to Zacharias because of the love he had for his sweet wife. The marvelous news he had for her hurried him home. His face still shone with wonder and excitement as he embraced Elisabeth. Something wonderful had happened! What was it? How mystified she was until her husband had finally written the whole wonderful story on his tablet. What good news! And Elisabeth *believed* it. She had often thought, in her longing for a child, of Sarah's son and of Rebekah's twins. She knew that nothing was impossible with God. Amazed and delighted, Elisabeth secluded herself for five months. We may be sure it was to ponder, to pray, and to praise God for His mercies, and to prepare for this child who was to do so much for his people. What a wonderful time these two old people had together—Elisabeth with her needle and Zacharias with his wax tablet and stylus—as they waited for the miraculous gift.

Elisabeth was a daughter of the priesthood and shared her husband's ideals and interests. Together they walked through life, righteous before God. They walked blamelessly obeying the "thou shalt nots" of His Word, but also living positive lives of faith doing good to all people. What more blessed thing can be said about married couples than that "they walked together." "Why is marriage so often a failure?" we ask. "Can two walk together, except they be agreed?" (Amos 3:3) is the divine key that unlocks the secret of happy marriages. Walking together as these two people had agreed to do—loving, sharing, and serving—makes marriage the most successful institution and the greatest blessing known to humankind.

Elisabeth's Cousin

As far as the neighbors could see, Mary was only a poor and obscure village girl who was honored to be a relative of the esteemed priest. They no doubt thought she had come to rejoice with her aged relative. But Elisabeth's faith saw in her youthful cousin the woman blessed above all others (Luke 1:42). With touching humility she said, "And whence is this to me, that the mother of my Lord should come to me?" (Luke 1:43).

No vanity, no selfish delight mars Elisabeth's character, even when her desire of a lifetime is about to be realized. In her, we see fine intellect inherited from her illustrious ancestry, ardent and constant piety, a great faith, a zeal for the honor of God, and a warm and generous heart. Only the fine sympathy and understanding that makes the joys and sorrows of another our own are visible between this aged saint and her young visitor. The months the cousins spent together were a pleasure to both for they had much to talk about and plan for. They had the Scriptures to search and God to praise for His special favors conferred upon them both.

Filled with the Holy Spirit, Elisabeth said, "There shall be a performance of those things which were told her from the Lord" (Luke 1:45). Mary returned to Galilee strengthened and comforted. Who knows how often these blessed women, with Joseph and Zacharias, little John and the holy child Jesus, met as the years went by. It can well be that they often visited together on feast days at Jerusalem. What precious fellowship must have been theirs!

Elisabeth's Son

Elisabeth soon rejoiced in the birth of her son. Her neighbors and relatives were surprised when she named him John. They said, "That cannot be right—the child must be named after his father!" How astonished they were when Zacharias wrote firmly, "His name is John." And they were astonished at the first words of Zacharias when he could speak again.

The story of the unusual events accompanying the birth of Elisabeth's son was told everywhere and the prophecy of Zacharias reported word for word. All wondered and were afraid. What kind of a child was this to be? A great priest? A prophet? Who knew? His parents knew only that he was appointed to do a great work (Luke 1:15–17), whatever that might involve. "Teach us what we shall do unto the child" (Judg. 13:8), must have been Elisabeth's daily prayer.

The child John grew robust, with the temperate habits of the Nazarene, and waxed strong in spirit under the religious training of his noble mother. It is thought that Elisabeth and Zacharias died while John was still young, but his mother lived long enough to impress upon the character of her son those qualities that so peculiarly marked her own.

Her strength of character, so noble and eloquent, was seen in her son, so that the people said, "Art thou Elijah? Art thou the Christ?" Like his mother, he was just and holy (Mark 6:20). The same faith, courage (Matt. 14:3–5), and zeal for God (John 5:35) lived on in her son. He fearlessly preached a different doctrine, the gospel of repentance and faith (John 3:35–36) and the necessity of a positive holy life (Luke 3:10–14).

John, "the grace or mercy of God," was the *voice* who introduced to those under the curse (Mal. 4:6) "the Lamb of God, which taketh away the sin of the world" (John 1:29).

When Jesus said, "Among them that are born of women there hath not risen a greater than John the Baptist" (Matt. 11:11), He honored Elisabeth for the part she had in John's greatness.

Every baby is wonderful. Every child is precious. Christ Himself attached an infinite price to a little child. We can learn from Elisabeth that it is the sacred obligation of Christian motherhood to acquaint the little ones with God's Word, to inspire them by a good example, to walk blameless before God, and to pass on to their children sanctified character traits. All children are inclined to sin and selfishness. It is every mother's solemn duty to curb bad traits in her children by teaching, restraint, and prayer, for these very qualities—good or bad—will shine in greater prominence in maturity.

The names of many prominent women glitter in history, but none with more radiant luster than that of believing Elisabeth. She attained the noblest virtues possible to women. How wonderful to know that every Christian woman can possess these same virtues by the grace of God. "Ye have not, because ye ask not" (James 4:2). The Truth and the Light of whom John bore witness that He was God's beloved Son, the One who honored Elisabeth said, "ask, and it shall be given you" (Matt. 7:7).

Suggestions for Discussion

1. Gabriel is God's special messenger of good news. See, for example, Daniel 9:20–23 and Luke 1:26–38. Was it unusual to be troubled by the sight of an angel (Judg. 6:22–23; 1 Chron. 21:30; Dan. 8:17, 27; Luke 2:9)?

2. Compare Luke 1:17 and Malachi 4:5–6.

3. Do you think that women today are as desirous of having children and pray as fervently for them as did Elisabeth?

4. Is it as easy to "walk together" today as it was for Elisabeth and her husband?

5. Often, relations between relatives are not as they should be. What can we learn from the visit of the cousins?

6. Considering that Elisabeth knew, to a certain extent, what

John's task would be, what do you think she told him? If he were your son, what would you have taught him? What part could Zacharias contribute to John's training?

7. Should we always train our children for great service?

8. Was there significance in the meaning of the name *John?* Explain. How did John die? About how old was he?

9. What good qualities did Elisabeth possess? Did she have any outstanding virtue?

10. Are most character traits inherited or acquired by daily contact with parents or others?

11. List and show from Scripture the character traits of John that remind you of his mother.

12. What was revolutionary about John's message? Where did John get his clear understanding of his mission?

And she . . . spake of him to all them that looked for redemption in Jerusalem.
—Luke 2:38

19

ᴬnna

Scripture Reading
Luke 2:21–38

ᴸuke's gospel narrative contains many stories, sayings, and parables found nowhere else. Inspired by the Holy Spirit, he wrote about the Master's work and was led to emphasize certain aspects of our Lord's teachings.

Jesus' understanding of women and sympathy with their needs impressed Luke. His attitude toward women was noble and uplifting. He gave them no special teaching, set before them no special ideal, but He admitted them into His kingdom on the same terms as He did men. In Christ "there is neither male nor female" (Gal. 3:28). He brought a new era to women, giving to them a place of usefulness and honorable service such as they had never had before. May it not be because of this that women were so irresistibly drawn toward the greatest of teachers, and followed and served the Man of Galilee with such humility and devotion?

The role of women in the life of our Lord is more prominent in the gospel of Luke than in the other Gospels. The birth and infancy narratives are told from the point of view of the women—Mary, Elisabeth, and Anna. The Christ was born of a woman (Gal. 4:4) and owed the care and early training of His childhood to a human mother. It was a woman, Elisabeth, who first confessed her faith in Jesus, and Anna welcomed the Savior into the world. Only Luke tells us about the group of women who, out of their own pockets, supplied the needs of Jesus and His disciples as they went from city to village preaching the gospel of salvation (Luke 8:1–3). In His hour of awful agony women clustered at the foot of the cross. Jesus saw them and expressed concern over His grieving mother. Only the women followed Joseph of Arimathea to see where the body of Jesus would be laid, and they prepared spices for His burial. They were last at the cross and first at the tomb, and the first words of the risen Lord were addressed, not to the disciples, but to a woman who "loved much." Women were among those praying in the Upper Room after the ascension, and they have been the most faithful members of the praying church ever since.

A Prophetess

Anna of Jerusalem was a prophetess. There had been a few others before her—godly, inspired women whose deeds were well known and whose very words were remembered. There had been Deborah and Miriam, and Huldah who lived in the college and was consulted by King Josiah on matters of importance. Anna was the last of these women who were known to be remarkably devout, habitual, and earnest in prayer, and having the gift of prophetic utterances. These Spirit-filled women were respected, and their advice was eagerly sought and honored.

In our modern era of specialized guidance and educated leadership, it remains true that those who live a consecrated life are still the most fit guides to others. Only those who walk in the light of God's presence, whether they are mothers in the home or women engaged in other activities, will shed the light of truth, peace, and hope into the lives of others.

Anna's family roots were in Asher, one of the dispersed tribes of Israel. When the people of Asher were given their portion in the land of Canaan, they did not drive out the enemy as God had required but "dwelt among the Canaanites." However, we read in 2 Chronicles 30 that when King Hezekiah restored the temple service and called the people to worship in Jerusalem, those of Asher did not jeer as some did but humbled themselves, turned to the Lord, and were blessed. Anna was one of the remnant of Israel, saved to serve and blessed to represent at Christ's coming the lost sheep of the house of Israel.

A Saint

We read of Anna only in Luke. In a brief description of her he tells us that she was an aged woman who had been a widow for about sixty years. Now, at eighty-four when she traveled back along the path of life, she remembered how rosy the future had been when she was a young woman. To be happily married to the man she loved was all any Jewish girl could ever want from life. But God, in love (though she did not understand it then), broke up her plans for earthly joy when He took away her husband after only seven years of married life. She knew, now that she was old, that it had been good for her to be afflicted. In her sorrow and loneliness she had turned to her Lord. She had set her affections on things above and had dedicated her life to her Maker, who was better to her than a husband. As time went by, her zeal and devotion to her precious Lord did not lessen but increased in intensity. Anna was steadfast, unmovable, always abounding in the work of the Lord, instructing others in the work of the Lord and in their sacred duties. She spoke to others of the coming of the Redeemer and of the restoration of Israel's glory.

There is a beauty and usefulness in old age, and even in middle age, that we do not generally appreciate. Most women dread middle age. How hard it is to relinquish youthful beauty and energy. Life is not over when the children grow up and leave home. For life as you have never enjoyed it—rich, broad, useful—may be just beginning! There is so much to do for others. There is always a drastic shortage of workers in the King's business.

What do you think Anna was doing at fifty? Trying desperately to keep her youth? Complaining that life had passed her by? What did she say at eighty? That she was "on the shelf" because she couldn't do her housecleaning or her own washing anymore? She had reached the years of strength when wisdom and faith had grown firm and sure, and she was busy night and day! She may have been a bit deaf, she may have had to peer close to the page of her Bible scroll, she may have walked slowly now, but she never missed a service in the temple. She was a familiar figure in the women's court, and it has been suggested that she had some work to do in the temple. It was a thrill for Anna to serve, even if it was just to trim the lamps. It could well be that she lived in the temple in one of the four rooms that were built in the corners of the women's court.

Moses, too, would have called Anna old (Ps. 90:10), but she was young in spirit. No one noticed her simple clothes or her thin arms and bent back. No one saw the lines in her sallow old face—only gentle sweetness and serenity that came from living in God's presence so constantly and so long. Anna lived in a difficult day. Life was drab and gray and hopeless for the great majority of the Jewish people, but Anna's face was radiant with an inner light, with a look of expectancy for great and blessed things to come. She was one of the few still waiting for the coming of the Redeemer. It is commonly said, "As long as there is life, there is hope." It is equally true that as long as there is hope, there is life. Anna's hope kept her busy, happy, interested in life and in the people around her.

A Missionary

Anna knew old Simeon well. She often met him as he passed through the court of the women on his way to the court of the Israelites. Venerable, devout, he too was one of the few who still looked for Israel's Redeemer. Simeon confidently expected to see

Him before he died! He, like Anna, had no attachment to this world and its pursuits; their hopes were toward God and their thoughts on immortality. They knew every prophecy from Isaiah to Malachi and looked every day for the Lord's Christ.

It was because Anna was faithful in God's house that she saw the Christ child. If she had made it a practice to stay at home for every ache in her old bones, for every sign of inclement weather, she would have missed Him. One day, there in the temple, she saw the One of whom the prophets had spoken. Her spirit stirred within her the moment she saw Mary cross the court with her Holy Child. Where did Simeon come from so quickly? His face was all rapture! Anna felt an irresistible urge to see what was unusual about the child that had so captivated Simeon. She hurried toward the little group—serious Joseph, the especially lovely and attractive young mother who was gazing wonderingly at her own child, aged Simeon lifting his face alight with praise. She reached Mary just as Simeon, with the Holy Child in his arms, blessed God, proclaiming that Christ was the light of the Gentiles and the glory of His people. Heedless of the baffled priest and the momentary hush of the curious crowd, Anna also gave thanks to God in tones tremulous with age and emotion. She understood, as Simeon did, that the Redeemer was to be the spiritual deliverer of *all* people. Even Isaiah (Isa. 62:2) was way ahead of the narrow, selfish school of Jesus' day who taught that the Messiah was only for the Jews. Anna understood because she enjoyed daily communion with God, searched the Scriptures, and found the truth. God's Word will change our lives very little if we seldom read it—or read it because we feel we should (John 5:39).

This was a glad day for Anna. Woman as well as man was to rejoice on the day of His coming. In the kingdom of our Lord there is no distinction of persons, of sex, of rank—all are one in Christ Jesus. There is no longer a court for the women to worship while the men approach close to the Holy Place. There is the inner chamber of prayer for all. The door of fruitful service and personal witness is open to women as well as men, and women are still among the most faithful of Christ's followers.

Unlike Simeon, who was ready to "depart in peace" now that he had seen the Messiah, Anna was stirred to action. She laid aside her prophetic robes and put on the garb of a missionary. Though burdened with the weakness and infirmities of old age, she proclaimed, far and near, the advent of the desire of nations. We can imagine her as with radiant face she told all who looked for the redemption of Israel: "Rejoice and be glad with me for the Messiah whom we have expected so long has come." She was certain that the child of Mary was the promised Savior because she was familiar with God, with grace, and with redemption. So, beginning at Jerusalem, Anna became the pioneer of a great company of women who publish the glad tidings (Ps. 68:11).

When, with the eye of faith, we have seen the Christ of God, we will give God praise and as Anna did, serve Him night and day. And while we wait with earnest expectation for the day when we shall see Him face to face, we must, "beginning at home," tell the glad story that we have been saved by grace. Our daily prayer will be:

> Lord, speak to me, that I may speak
>   In living echoes of Thy tone;
> As Thou has sought, so let me seek
>   Thy erring children lost and lone.
>
> O, use me, Lord, use even me,
>   Just as Thou wilt, and when, and where;
> Until Thy blessed face I see,
>   Thy rest, Thy joy, Thy glory share.
>   —Frances Havergal

Suggestions for Discussion

1. As you read and study from the book of Luke, notice the many women mentioned. Why do you think women figure so prominently in Luke's gospel?
2. What did Christianity do for women?

3. In what ways did Anna represent her people when she welcomed the Savior?

4. Compare the reactions of Simeon and Anna as their hopes were realized.

5. Name some blessings enjoyed by older people who have served the Lord throughout their lives.

6. Do elderly people outlive their usefulness? Explain.

7. How can every one of us be a missionary? Where should we begin our witnessing? Why?

8. Name some women missionaries who have gone out from your own church.

9. What do we find easier to share—gossip or the gospel?

10. Women who have had children often have much less to do when they reach middle age because their children have left home to be married, and so forth. Do you think they should "take it easy" or find new avenues of service? How and where can older women serve best?

11. How do we see Jesus? What should be the expectation of every Christian?

12. This lesson has special interest for older women, but those who are young will also one day be older. What can we learn from this lesson of Anna?

Lord, dost thou not care that my sister hath left me to serve alone?
—Luke 10:40

20

Martha

Scripture Reading
Luke 10:38–42; John 11:1–46; 12:1–2

℃hristian hospitality is a virtue. From ancient days, it has been considered a sacred duty to receive, feed, and lodge any stranger who might stop at the door. A stranger was treated as a guest, and those who had eaten together had a strong claim on one another's friendship and loyalty. Moses told the Israelites that it was their religious duty to show hospitality: "Love ye therefore the stranger . . . and the stranger . . . shall eat and be satisfied" (Deut. 10:19; 14:29). The stranger was called to rejoice in the blessings God gave to his host (Deut. 26:11). Job said, "The stranger did not lodge in the street: but I opened my doors to the traveler" (Job 31:32), and God said that Job was perfect and upright.

True hospitality is "love of the stranger"; it is sharing what we have. To share of our abundance is pleasant and easy, but to share of our little requires trust in our heavenly Father. The widow of Zarephath shared her little with Elijah and the Lord supplied her needs. Thousands of years ago a great woman showed hospitality to Elisha. She said, "Let us make a little chamber, I pray thee, on the wall; and let us set for him there a bed, and a table, and a stool, and a candlestick: and it shall be, when he cometh to us, that he shall turn in thither" (2 Kings 4:10). How blessed are the homes in which this spirit of "love to the stranger" is found.

The spirit of Christian hospitality is taught in the New Testament by Jesus and His followers in Luke 14:12–14; Titus 1:8; and 1 Peter 4:9. Hospitality is commendable in anyone, but it is a *necessary* virtue for a Christian. One day when Jesus was speaking of the final judgment he said, "And the King shall answer . . . , Depart from me, ye cursed, into everlasting fire, prepared for the devil and his angels: . . . I was a stranger, and ye took me not in" (Matt. 25:40–41, 43).

Abraham was "not forgetful to entertain strangers" and thereby "entertained angels unawares" (Heb. 13:2). Martha was hostess to the Altogether Lovely One whom the angels worshiped. *Did Martha entertain Him unawares?*

Managing Martha

Bethany, where Martha lived, was a small, pleasant village nestled on the eastern slope of Mount Olivet near the Jericho Road, Bethphage, and Bethlehem. It was a short pleasant walk of two miles over the south tip of Olivet to Jerusalem. Martha could follow the footpath to the crest of the hill and, on a clear day, see the rays of the bright sun turn the mass of gold and snowy marble that was the temple to a blaze of glory.

Martha, her sister, and her brother had a comfortable and attractive home surrounded with palms and shrubbery. The expensive ointment that Martha's sister lavished on Jesus would indicate that this Bethany family was well-to-do. The fact that many Jews came from Jerusalem to visit and stay with the mourning sisters shows that the family was of some wealth and social importance. The home evidently belonged to Martha, and it is possible that she was the widow of Simon the leper (Matt. 26:6; John 12:1–2).

The family at Bethany had a wonderful friend, Jesus of Nazareth. When He was in the vicinity of Jerusalem He made Martha's house His home, and He did not hesitate to bring His disciples with Him, for they found loyal friends and generous hospitality there. Whenever the scribes, the Pharisees, and doctors made it difficult for Jesus with their ridicule and contempt, whenever He was worn and weary, when His great heart ached with the burdens of humanity, He could walk to Bethany and find a haven of rest, hearts that believed in Him and were attuned to His.

Jesus spent much time on the Mount of Olives. Under its olive trees He rested and prayed. In its shady groves He sat to teach His disciples. From its hillside He yearned over Jerusalem and predicted its destruction. On its western slope was the Garden of Gethsemane, and in its dark shadows He was betrayed. At the base of Olivet His triumphal entrance into Jerusalem began, and from its summit He ascended into glory. Jesus often must have gone from the mountain into the warmth and fellowship of the home of His friends, for, from Martha's familiarity with Jesus, we conclude that she knew Him well.

Martha was a good manager and hard worker, and her home was always spotlessly clean and attractive. Martha was the kind of woman we would make chairman of an important committee or president of a ladies group. Not a project would fail, no committee would lag with managing Martha as chairman. No other banquets were held like the kind Martha supervised! All of Bethany knew how capable she was, and when they needed advice or help with a supper or village project, they called on her and she spared neither time nor energy, for she was a generous, able woman.

At the time our story opens, Martha is busy preparing a sumptuous meal in her own home. The guest of honor is Jesus, and the best produce of the Jerusalem markets is none too good for her special friend. We visualize Martha bustling about with an apron on, flecking off a speck of dust, capably giving orders to the servants—then testing the cakes herself—rearranging the silver correctly, appraising the angle of the couches, her face warm and pink from bending over the steaming pots.

How different the quiet, contemplative Mary was from her older sister Martha. Their personalities were poles apart! Even now, while Martha was in a dither over the dinner, Mary calmly sat and chatted with their guest! It irritated busy bustling Martha to see her sister doing nothing, especially on a day like this when there was so much serving to do. Jesus had sent many disciples out on a preaching tour. They were now coming back to see Jesus at Martha's house, so she had many supper guests and everyone was welcome. Perhaps more came than she had planned for or something went wrong in the kitchen. Martha was tired and tense and, in a burst of displeasure, she suddenly confronted Jesus where He was relaxing in the pleasant, shady courtyard. With a curt turn toward her sister, who was listening intently to the Master, Martha blurted, "Why is Mary sitting here doing nothing while I am swamped with work? Tell her to help me!" Martha was no longer managing her work; her work was managing Martha! There was a tinge of jealousy, too, in the busy heart of Martha as she reproved both Mary and her Master.

It was in Martha's courtyard, under the shade of her own olive tree, that Jesus preached a great sermon to her and to all modern Marthas who are in a constant dither over housekeeping to the exclusion of the other good things of life. Jesus said, "Martha, Martha, thou art careful and troubled about many things" (Luke 10:41). Surely, Martha's attitude toward her work was wrong, for it left her frustrated and peevish. Also a more simple meal, leaving time for fellowship with her Great Guest, would have been better for Martha.

It was not that Martha did not love her Lord. It was she who invited Him and then provided Him with every comfort, generously giving of her strength and substance. Jesus did not reprove Martha for her industry—He believed in working hard and said, "My Father worketh hitherto, and I work" (John 5:17). The Lord did not chide her for lack of generosity, loyalty, or love, but for being anxious and worried "about a multitude of things." Jesus knew the futility and evil of worry and how it takes the joy out of life.

Jesus loved Martha and was appreciative of her services, but Martha needed to learn that there were also other ways of serving the Lord that are even more pleasing to Him. He said, "Mary hath chosen that good part. . . ." What a surprise that must have been for loving and capable Martha.

When Martha's eyes were opened, she learned that a good hostess must strive to keep that rare balance between the kitchen and fellowship with the family and with the Ever-Present Guest. Later, at a supper in Simon's house, Martha quietly served (John 12:1–2), and she listened intently now to the immortal words of Jesus. Her heart was as full of gratitude and love as Mary's was when she anointed the feet of her Master.

Mourning Martha

A touchingly beautiful story of Martha's home in sorrow is found in John 11. Here we see the humanity of Jesus in the brief but dramatic words, "Jesus wept" (John 11:35). We are deeply stirred by the love and compassion of the "friend that sticketh closer than a brother" (Prov. 18:24). We learn from this story that suffering makes a house a home, for it brings out tenderness and understanding, appreciation of family and friends as nothing else can.

When the family at Bethany entertained Jesus at dinner, Mary was commended for having chosen "that good part." But when the home of the sisters was unexpectedly plunged into sorrow, it was Martha who stood out with the majesty of a woman who could meet life's trials and not be crushed by them.

Both sisters lovingly cared for Lazarus when he was ill. But we are sure that Martha, still the manager, was the one who brought out the remedies, made the decisions, and, when the seriousness of his illness became apparent, sent the urgent appeal to Jesus, "He whom thou lovest is sick" (John 11:3). They had been so sure that the Great Physician would come, but He had not, and now the brother they loved was dead. Again, it was Martha who made arrangements for the funeral and the seven-day mourning vigil. Now

Lazarus was laid in the tomb. How often the sorrowing sisters said to one another and to their friends, "If only Jesus had come!"

Mary was overcome with grief, but Martha could shift the weight of her sorrow by keeping occupied with work. Martha still watched for Jesus among the crowds on the street. Many times a day she glanced at the footpath up Olivet and peered toward the Jericho road. What a relief when at last He came! Without a word to her sister, Martha slipped out of the house to meet Jesus at the edge of the village. In a burst of excited feeling she said, as soon as she saw Him, "Lord, if thou hadst been here, my brother had not died" (John 11:21). There was disappointment in Martha's voice, a hint of the manager in what she said, but hers was also the simple language of faith and love. She had faith in the Miracle Worker of Galilee, and when she was in His presence she knew intuitively that nothing was impossible for Him. Now Martha talked with the Teacher about the great truths of redemption (John 11:24–27), and when Jesus asked "Believest thou this?" there was triumphant faith in Martha's answer. Her reply is one of the most beautiful confessions of faith in all of the New Testament.

Martha was a woman of impulse, energy, and practical duty. Like Peter she was ready to give advice, to put everyone in his or her place, even her Lord. Like Peter she made a great confession when she called Jesus the Lord of her life, the promised Messiah, the Son of God.

After this Jesus asked to see Mary. Martha, considerate and compassionate of her sister, called her out of the house secretly so that she might have a moment alone with Jesus, but crowds of sympathetic Jews followed Mary, thinking she was going to the tomb to weep there. When Jesus saw Mary's sorrow and heard the cries of the mourners, His loving heart ached with compassion, and "Jesus wept." *Surely He hath borne our griefs, and carried our sorrows* (Isa. 53:4).

Now, with Mary and Martha beside Him and with many Jews from Jerusalem watching, He performed His last great miracle. When Jesus said, "Roll away the stone from the grave," Martha was quick once again to advise even her Lord. Jesus patiently and lovingly said, "Have faith, Martha, and you shall see the glory of the Lord!"

Bringing Lazarus back to life confirmed the faith of Martha. It filled the hearts of the sisters of Bethany with thankfulness and undying devotion to the Great Guest who honored their home with His presence. It made their loving hearts His eternal dwelling place.

Behold how Jesus loved Martha, her sister, and Lazarus!

Suggestions for Discussion

1. What is Christian hospitality? Look up the following passages: Luke 14:12–14; Romans 12:13; Titus 1:8; Hebrews 13:2; and 1 Peter 4:9.
2. How do we exercise hospitality today?
3. How does Martha find her counterpart in modern women?
4. How can we come to the conclusion that Martha and her family were well known and better off than many of their neighbors?
5. Why did Jesus rebuke Martha?
6. How do we know that Jesus does not want us to worry?
7. How does worry hurt us? Others? Jesus? What reason did Martha have for believing that Jesus could restore Lazarus?
8. Are there any blessings in sorrow?
9. Point out where Martha showed her strength, weakness, generosity, loyalty, faith, hope, love, consideration, and courage.

*Wheresoever this gospel shall be preached through-
out the whole world, this also that she hath done
shall be spoken of for a memorial of her.*
—Mark 14:9

21

Mary
of Bethany

Scripture Reading
Matthew 26:6–13; Mark 14:3–9;
Luke 10:38–42; John 11:1–2, 19–20,
30–36, 45; 12:1–9

A gift is defined as something freely given from
one person to another without any compensation and without any
agreement or contract. A gift or present is something given as an
expression of affection, friendship, or respect for another. The perfect example is God's great gift, freely given because God so loved
the world. No one on earth, nor all those who ever lived, can together compensate for the gift of the Savior.

Every year in December we celebrate this greatest of all events,
and in various ways we try to show our thankfulness to the Lord
for the gift of His only begotten Son. We are influenced, however,
and often sidetracked by the way Christmas is celebrated in our
country. Christmas, originally a religious holiday, has been

increasingly commercialized. There is no other occasion during the year that can be used to such advantage by the retail industry. Old Saint Nicholas is the jolly partner of this industry. There is an annual urge, extending over many weeks, to send lists to Santa and make gift selections early. Though Christians do not believe in Santa, they have done very little to check his influence.

Many have adopted the Christmas list idea for various reasons. When we make our Christmas lists do we plan to give or to get? Do we freely give, or is our aim a profitable exchange? Jesus said "If ye do good to them which do good to you, what thank have ye?" (Luke 6:33). Rather, "sell that thou hast, and give to the poor" (Matt. 19:21). Then, like the wise men, we would be bringing gifts to Jesus, for whatever we give to the needy we give to Him.

There is also a personal gift that we can give directly to Jesus. Christina Rossetti tells us about this kind of gift when she says:

> What can I give Him,
>   Poor as I am?
> If I were a shepherd
>   I would bring a lamb.
> If I were a wise man
>   I would do my part,
> Yet what I can I give Him,
>   Give Him my heart.

Give me your heart says the Father above. No gift is so precious to Him as our love. And that is what Mary, the sister of Martha and Lazarus did—she gave her heart to the Christ of Christmas.

Quiet in Meditation

There are no more interesting character sketches in the Bible than those of the two sisters of Bethany. We have an intimate look into their home. We see their devotion to one another and to the Lord whom they love and serve, each in her own way. It is a story that will live forever. Jesus Himself said to Mary, "Wherever my story is told, yours will be told also."

We feel as if we actually know Mary and Martha. Perhaps they are so familiar to us because we find their counterpart in ourselves. We find that their faults and peculiarities, their qualities and temperaments are much like our own.

There is much in us of the Martha—bustling, busy, but well-intentioned. Work can become a feverish activity, and we can be taken up in its fast pace. Even our religious life is no exception, for there is much zealous activity to do good. Among women, much kingdom service is accomplished by a busy, circuitous route. The dollar we give seems to take on added value when it is turned into raw material and then sold again. So, much ado is made about giving and, like Martha, we are apt to be a bit critical of those who serve the Lord in other ways than we do.

When Jesus visited His friends in their home in Bethany, He was entertained at a dinner. The hostess, efficient, practical Martha had planned a delicious meal. So much effort had gone into the preparations that she was feverish with excitement. She was tired, anxious, and tense. At the same time, Mary was apparently relaxing and enjoying herself.

We know that Mary was a good listener, quiet and contemplative, for we read in Luke 10:39, "And she had a sister called Mary, which also sat at Jesus' feet, and heard his word." Mary had a hungry soul and sat humbly as a pupil before her Teacher. She was so absorbed in the wonderful words of life that she was completely oblivious to all the fussing and fuming of her sister—even Martha's disapproving looks did not penetrate. Mary's whole attention was focused on her heavenly Visitor who "spoke as never man spoke before." He talked with authority and tenderness. His voice was like the mellow music of a harp. Mary had only to touch His heartstrings and she heard the voice of infinite love and understanding. Martha loved Jesus, too, but in her anxiety to serve Him she heard only the bubbling of pots and the clanging of pans.

There is nothing that so illustrates the characters of the two sisters as when Martha, instead of gently calling Mary, irritably said, "Lord, dost thou not care that my sister hath left me to serve alone? bid her therefore that she help me. And Jesus answered and said to her, Martha, Martha, thou art careful and troubled about many things: But one thing is needful; and Mary hath chosen that good part, which shall not be taken away from her" (Luke 10:40–42). Mary had a quiet temperament. Even when Martha's sharp tongue lashed out at her, she said nothing. To be quiet under provocation is a gift for which all women should pray. It was a quality the Master Himself possessed (Isa. 53:7).

Mary, too, entertained Jesus. But, being a spiritually sensitive woman, she knew even better than her older sister what Jesus needed most. Jesus was physically and mentally worn with the unrelenting demands of the multitudes. Wherever He walked He was pushed and pressed by the curious crowds. He sometimes climbed into a boat, pushed away from the milling masses, and taught His disciples while the wavelets gently rocked His boat. In Jerusalem He was especially harassed by verbal and pointed challenges of His truth and mission. He was human. He knew utter weariness of body and spirit, and He needed understanding and fellowship. This Mary gave Him, and He loved her the more tenderly for it.

Mary chose the good part—the place at His feet and close to His heart. If there is anything we need today it is time for meditation and fellowship with Jesus. We say so readily, "I can't take time for the quiet hour even though I know I need it," or more often we simply say, "I'm too busy." It is just those who are too busy, those under the pressure of hurried, anxious living that need quiet times for sitting at Jesus' feet where problems, like burdens, can be laid down. All the things with which we are so busy today will one day be gone, but faith in Christ and fellowship with Him will be a part of our eternal happiness.

Mary was quiet in sorrow. When trial came to her she could sit still and ponder. We read that after Lazarus died, "Mary sat still in the house," while Martha was as busy as ever. Mary had a tender sympathetic heart and was deeply affected by the death of her brother. Though she was grief stricken she did not fret or complain because she knew that Jesus was her Lord, and if He had wanted it otherwise He would have come in time to save her brother's life.

In many ways Mary was a woman of deep, intense feelings. It appears that she was especially attached to her brother, for the friends from Jerusalem came to comfort Mary (John 11:31, 45). Her friends loved her, and it was always restful and relaxing to be with her—even in sorrow she was an inspiration. No one seemed to notice when Martha slipped out of the house to meet Jesus, but as soon as Mary left they followed her. They wanted to be with her every moment.

When Mary sobbed out her sorrow at Jesus' feet, she did not add a word of complaint or suggestion as Martha had done but humbly expressed her faith in His love and power. Jesus spoke words of comfort to Martha. But when Mary came to Him, her heart brimming with sorrow, Jesus wept with sympathy more eloquent than words.

Quiet in Devotion

The third and last scene in which Mary figures prominently is at a supper in Bethany at the home of Simon the leper. Perhaps Simon, a long-time leper, had been healed by Jesus and wanted to show his appreciation. Or, the dinner may have been given to rejoice with Lazarus who had been raised from the dead only a few days before, for both Jesus and Lazarus were guests of honor.

It took courage to entertain Jesus that week before His death. The raising of Lazarus from the dead had caused such an angry stir among the Jews that the chief priest had called a special assembly of the Sanhedrin, and there Caiaphas the high priest said that it was expedient that Jesus should die (John 11:50). They also considered putting Lazarus to death, for because of him many Jews believed in Jesus. The fury of the enemies of Jesus was rapidly reaching its climax, and this very evening a disciple was to give the final impetus that would lead to His death.

It appears that the dinner was for men only. Close friends of

Jesus and His disciples were there—surely John, James, Matthew, Thomas, and we know Judas was at the table. Lazarus, who only a few days before had been dead and sealed in a tomb, was the center of attention. Skillful, hardworking Martha was serving the meal. This is what she could do best and she loved to do it, especially on this glad occasion when she could show her thankfulness to Jesus for restoring her brother.

Nor did Mary desert Jesus when the danger was the greatest. She came to the supper because all those she loved the most were there. She, too, wanted to show her gratitude to Jesus. She had much for which to be thankful. Sitting at His feet, she had learned many spiritual lessons. He had given back her brother, and she had found in Jesus a completely understanding friend and recognized Him as her Lord. He had given to her the divine love that excels all other love. Mary's heart was so full of grateful love that she was compelled to express it. A great love must always find expression no matter what the cost.

Mary—poised, pure, and meek—came softly behind Jesus where He was reclining on a couch at the dinner table. First one guest then another looked up as Mary broke the seal on a beautiful alabaster flask. There was a hush in the room—some of the men were curious, others critical, at least one was angry—while they watched Mary pour the precious nard* on the head of Jesus. From His hair it dripped down on His seamless robe, and from the robe it ran down on His feet. The sweet spikenard filled the room with a heavy fragrance. In complete devotion, Mary untied her lovely long hair and with it, humbly and adoringly, wiped the excess of perfume from His feet. When, a few days later, the Roman soldiers pressed the crown of thorns on Jesus, the King of the Jews, Mary's spikenard was still in His hair, and when the soldier held His seamless robe it

---

*Spikenard was an aromatic ointment that was extracted from an East Indies plant. It was rare and expensive. The pound in use among the Jews was the Roman weight of twelve ounces. It sold for three hundred pence, which was about equivalent to a year's wages.

still diffused the sweet smell, the unusual gift of Mary's devotion.

So Mary brought her rare and costly gift to her Lord. He approved of her gift, for when the disciples, Judas in particular, called it a waste, Jesus said, "Let her alone: against the day of my burying hath she kept this" (John 12:7). Though the disciples were critical at first, they were so impressed with this incident that later Matthew, Mark, and John all wrote in detail about it (John 11:2 indicating the importance attached to it).

Mary showed evidence of knowing more of His secret power and mission than even His disciples. She had heard Him speak of His death, and she knew that some things were worth dying for. In her eyes whatever He did was right. Mary, impassioned and pensive, is perhaps the most spiritually sensitive woman in the New Testament.

Mary's gift was beautiful in its motive, in its abandon of self, in its quiet devotion. Many others had done things for Jesus—some gave food and money, some lent Him their boats, another his colt, and one his grave—but the only deed on which Christ pronounced immortal fame was the gift of Mary of Bethany, who had first given her heart to Him and then had given the most precious gift her imaginative mind could design.

Like Mary, who was quiet in meditation, we must choose the better part. We must, in time of trial, "be still and know that He is God"; in time of provocation and criticism let God be our Judge. Because true love must find expression, we will give our Lord the best we have—our hearts and our gifts in endless devotion.

Suggestions for Discussion

1. Do you think that Mary was the type of woman who would leave her sister with all the work?
2. What is that good part which Mary chose? How can we obtain that good part? How much do we need it? Can we share it? How?
3. Who defended Mary against Martha's accusation? What

could Mary have said in her own defense? What does this
teach us about Mary's character, and what practical lesson
do we find here for ourselves?

4. Does Jesus' approval of Mary's way of serving Him mean
that hers is the only approved way?

5. What does it mean that Mary was quiet in sorrow?

6. Is there any significance in the fact that Mary's name alone
is mentioned in John 11:31 and 45?

7. Both sisters came to Jesus with their sorrow. How did
Jesus react to and help each one?

8. How would being a Martha or a Mary affect our home life?
Is it possible to be both?

9. Did anointing the feet of Jesus have anything to do with
custom (e.g., Luke 7:46; John 13:5)? What was the
significance of Mary's anointing of Jesus?

10. Who criticized Mary for being lavish? See Matthew 26:8;
Mark 14:4; and John 12:5. Is criticism contagious?
Explain.

11. Do we need more women to put on dinners to make
money for charity, missions, and so on, or more women
who donate generously and quietly? Which is the better
way to give?

12. What exactly is personality? Describe Mary's personality.

13. Why was Mary's gift so outstanding that she merited both
the approval of Jesus and the memorial of being
remembered as long as the gospel is preached throughout
the whole world?

*And she, being before instructed of her mother, said,
Give me here John Baptist's head in a charger.*
—Matthew 14:8

22

Herodias

and Her Daughter

Scripture Reading
Matthew 14:1–12; Mark 6:17–30;
Luke 3:19–20

"Parents, if you desire honor be worthy" stands out boldly on an illuminated billboard of a modern church in one of our large cities. This saying represents the latest approach to the troublesome problem of parent-child-school relationships.

Parents have been swayed the last two decades by popular child-training concepts and have followed the easy method of letting children do as they please. Children were invested with imaginary maturity, and they could choose for themselves whether they would study in school or just get by. They need give account of themselves to parents or superiors only if they were so inclined. Lack of restrictions and parental control have led to serious problems both in the school and in the home.

Schools, perhaps because they were blamed first, rallied to the cause of the problem child. To meet the needs of the teenager and to prevent the spread of delinquency, schools expanded their programs by adding such courses as safe driving, good grooming, and how to get along with the opposite sex. They also added clinics and various character-building enterprises. After going overboard on sports and extracurricular activities, schools slowly came to realize that trying to do good for everybody did good for nobody. All this time child study centers, child-psychiatric clinics, probation and parole associations, social workers, and educators tussled with the American child's behavior problems. School problem commissions were appointed, panels were popular, children were interviewed and their words of wisdom on the problem of juvenile delinquency were printed and broadcast. Today, educators have decided again that their real job is to impart intellectual knowledge—with the emphasis on the three Rs.

The result to date has been to bring the blame home to the parents. A subtle suggestion has been made that we might need a Parents Anonymous to do what AA does for alcoholics. Parents are told not to ruin the child with kindness, that children do need a firm hand and can profit after all by the mature wisdom and loving authority of parents. Now parents are blamed for the misbehavior of their children. When youthful enthusiasm goes out of bounds after a football game, it is suggested that parents be punished; for if parents do not teach their children respect for the property of others, the parents should be made to pay.

Behavior specialists occasionally pick rules for conduct from the Bible, and the words of wisdom on the church billboard are based on Christian principles. Worthy parents are the best example of how to get along with the opposite sex. They have daily opportunity to teach honesty, fair play, and respect for authority. Parents set the standard of morality and, day by day, provide the measure of values. However, parents often underestimate their own influence or do not seriously and prayerfully try to be worthy.

Basic to good family and social relationships is God's perfect law of love. God's Word tells us to love God above all and be "kindly affectioned one to another with brotherly love; in honor preferring one another" (Rom. 12:10) and that love works no ill to his neighbor. The Eternal Ruler tells us to show respect for authority. Render, therefore, to all their dues—fear to whom fear, honor to whom honor. It is all-important to know that love is the fulfilling of the Law. By these rules Christian parents build character; by their life they prove their own worthiness or failure.

There was no respect for God or love for others in the heart of Herodias. She had no genuine concern for the future of her only child, Salome, and proved herself a mother unworthy of honor.

Her Wicked Family

Herodias is called the Jezebel of the New Testament. Like Jezebel, who was the power behind the throne of wicked but weak Ahab, Herodias brought out all that was evil in wicked but irresolute Herod. Yet God in His inscrutable wisdom allowed Herodias a place in the gallery of well-known women.

Sacred history records only one incident in the life of Herodias—the story of the beheading of John the Baptist—but mentions every important member of the depraved Herod family. Each one played a significant role in that dramatic era of world history when the Son of God came to conquer sin and to lay the cornerstone and foundation of the Christian church.

All of the Herods, from Herod the Great, instigator of the Bethlehem massacre, to the fourth generation, who were identified with the government of Palestine, are mentioned in the New Testament. After Herod the Great came his sons Herod Archelaus (Matt. 2:22), Herod Antipas, and Herod Philip II (Luke 3:1); then Herod Agrippa I (Acts 12:1) and Herod Agrippa II, before whom Paul made his memorable defense (Acts 25:13–27). Antipas, the husband of Herodias, is mentioned more often in the New Testament than any other Herod.

We are indebted to Josephus, a Jewish historian who lived at the time of the apostles, for the detailed history of the Herods. He tells us that Herod the Great was the grandfather of Herodias. He was known to be a horribly wicked but powerful despot who died soon after the birth of Jesus. He had ten wives and murdered Mariamne who was the only wife he ever loved. When Herod became suspicious (which suspicions were entirely unfounded) that Mariamne, her two brothers, and his own son were plotting against him, Herod killed them all in a jealous rage. When the Magi asked him, "Where is he that is born King of the Jews?" (Matt. 2:2), his jealous spirit was so aroused that he sought "the young child to destroy him" (Matt. 2:13).

The family roots of the Herods were in the Edomites and each possessed all the crafty, jealous, cruel, and revengeful traits of Herod the Great. Herodias, daughter of murdered Aristobulus and niece of Mariamne, married Antipas, who ruled over the tetrarchy of Galilee and Perea (one-fourth of the territory over which his father had ruled). He was sly and ambitious, but not as able as his father. Herodias, who possessed all the evil traits of her notorious family, took advantage of him.

Her New City

Herodias lived in a city that her husband had built on the southwest side of the Sea of Galilee (also called Gennesaret or the Sea of Tiberias). He named the city Tiberius after Caesar and made it the capital of Galilee. From where she lived, Herodias could see the harp-shaped lake set like a burnished mirror in a framework of camel-colored hills. The sea, which the Master of the winds and waves once calmed, was often like her own tempestuous heart.

Crafty, ambitious, alert to the political atmosphere, she must have heard of Galilee's newest sensation, the miracle-working prophet. Herod heard of Jesus (Mark 6:14), and his steward Chuza's wife, Joanna, was one of the women who ministered to the needs of Jesus (Luke 8:3). Jesus often stayed in nearby Capernaum at the home of the fisherman Peter. He had chosen some of His disciples from this region, and many great miracles were performed within a few miles of the home of Herodias. Though we do not read of Jesus ever entering Tiberius, we do know that people from the city followed Him on foot and by boat to the other side of the lake where the miracle of the loaves was performed (John 6). How near Herodias lived to the eternal King, but how far she was from His kingdom!

Her Courageous Enemy

The enemy of sensuous Herodias was the fearless preacher, John the Baptist, who represented holiness and truth.

Herodias first had been married to her uncle Philip, and a daughter, whom Josephus calls Salome, was born to them. Philip was retired to Rome by Herod the Great for his supposed collaboration with Philip's mother, Mariamne. Historians say that Herod and his wife, Areta of Arabia, visited with Herodias and her husband in Rome. Herod and Herodias were immediately attracted to each other. Herod was drawn to her proud beauty and strength of personality. Herodias, not content with a quiet life with Philip, wanted rank, wealth, and magnificence. Herod, also her uncle, was the greatest prince in the family. She was ambitious and greedy and wanted nothing less than a queen's crown—sin and scandal meant nothing to her.

When Areta saw what was happening, she returned to Arabia. Herodias quickly divorced Philip and, with her dancing daughter, went to Tiberius with Herod. This marriage was offensive to the Jews because it was both illicit and incestuous.

Who dared to reprove immoral, unscrupulous Herod? Only one like John (Mark 6:18) who, in the spirit and power of Elias, would turn the hearts of the disobedient to the wisdom of the just (Luke 1:17). And how Herodias hated John! She would have murdered him at once, but Herod prevented her because he was afraid of the reaction of the people who believed that John was a great prophet. Herod himself was fascinated by the holy and just preacher and listened to him in many things. To punish John, and perhaps to protect him from his vindictive wife, Herod had John chained in the gloomy dungeon of Machaerus in Perea.

Her Dancing Daughter

Herodias did not forget but waited for revenge. When Herod celebrated his birthday in the palace his father had built in the fortress in Machaerus, her opportunity came.

It was a wild, but luxurious and sumptuous, banquet. The tetrarch was flattered by the fawning attentions of his Galilean nobles and high-ranking officers, and all were well intoxicated when a surprise number appeared on the program. Pretty teenage Salome, the daughter of Herodias, danced into the banquet hall. According to some she danced with many veils that she gracefully flung off, one by one. Her dance was wild, exotic, indecent, and unbecoming before a group of inebriated men. The guests were delighted. Herod was beside himself with pride and pleasure.

In his excitement, Herod rashly offered Salome anything she wanted. Salome was thrilled and quickly consulted her wicked mother. In a moment she was back (Mark 6:25) demanding that her gift be the head of John the Baptist on a platter.

Herod was shocked into soberness. If the princess had asked for a golden coach and a pair of Arabian bays he would have been pleased. He was sorry. But, out of a false sense of honor and because of the power a wicked woman had over his life, he granted her request. Salome, who was the tool of her mother, accepted the gory gift of the head of John on a golden platter from the banquet table and hurried with it to Herodias who received it with inhuman pleasure.

By training, counsel, and example, Herodias had led her daughter into sin. We should never underestimate the power of a woman over a man for good or for evil, nor should we forget that maternal influence is always eternal in its implications. Do we realize what a tremendous responsibility belongs to wives and mothers?

Salome's dancing became the symbol of her way of life, and her story has ever been a warning to the Christian church. Many churches have forbidden dancing chiefly because of the passions that are aroused by the dance and the other evils that may ensue.

From Josephus we learn that Salome married Herod Philip II, and we are told that she met a horrible death.

We wonder if Herodias was with Herod in the judgment hall where Jesus was mocked. If she was, her life was not touched by Him for she was evil to the end. Once more she reached for power when, because of jealousy of her brother Agrippa, she induced Herod to go to Rome and demand a crown. When they met Caesar their evil deeds were disclosed. Herod was divested of his tetrarchy, and they were banished to Gaul where they died in ignominy and poverty.

Herodias desired nothing as much as worldly honor, but instead she has gone down in history as the most sinful and dishonorable of women.

Suggestions for Discussion

1. What does this mean: "Parents if you desire honor be worthy?"
2. In your opinion, who should pay for the misdemeanors of children (e.g., destruction of another's property, car accidents, and so on): parents or the children? Where does respect for the things of others begin?
3. In what ways can parents sometimes be poor examples in respect to authority?
4. Is there significance in the fact that the most wicked family of rulers the world has ever known were in power when God sent His Son into the world?
5. What did Jesus call Herod (Luke 13:32)?
6. What did John tell Herod? How did the Jews feel about adultery and divorce?
7. Who was the more disturbed about John's accusation, Herod or Herodias? Why?
8. Why was Herod afraid to kill John? What does Matthew say? Luke?
9. It is thought that Jesus never went into Tiberius. Could there have been a reason?

10. Can you recall an instance in the Old Testament where a woman refused to do what Salome did?
11. What position does the church take in respect to dancing?
12. Define the character of Herodias. Could Christian women have any of these qualities?
13. Do you think that Herodias could have influenced Herod to let Jesus go when He was before Herod for judgment?
14. What is the moral of the story of Herodias and her daughter?

Then came she and worshipped him, saying, Lord, help me.
—Matthew 15:25

23

The Syrophoenician Woman

Scripture Reading
Matthew 15:21–28; Mark 7:24–30

$\mathscr{A}$s Christians, we have been well taught that ours is a world and life view. We sing of the faith of our forebears and are proud of our glorious heritage. We stand foursquare upon the gospel tenets and believe that faith without works is dead. As Paul would say, "Lest any man should boast" (Eph. 2:9). And James boldly challenges, "What doth it profit, my brethren, though a man say he hath faith, and have not works?" (James 2:14).

We agree with James that it is more important to see faith in action than to boast or talk, however eloquently, about it. We believe that the gospel of the kingdom has social implications and obligations. Jesus Himself clearly taught us, both by example and precept, that He came to preach the gospel *and to show mercy* to those in need (Matt. 4:23; 9:35; and so on). The Gospels are replete with stories of healing. We read again and again ". . . and they were healed . . . and [he] healed them all" (Luke 6:18–19).

Showing mercy to the sick and needy was a large part of the Savior's blessed ministry. When John's disciples came to inquire of Jesus whether He was the Messiah, He sent this message to John: "The blind receive their sight, and the lame walk, the lepers are cleansed, and the deaf hear, the dead are raised up, and the poor have the gospel preached to them" (Matt. 11:5).

The Lord's commission to the twelve disciples, and again to the seventy, was to preach the kingdom of God and to heal the sick (Mark 3:14–15; Luke 9:2; 10:9), and they obeyed Him (Luke 9:6). Christ left us a perfect example, and we should follow in His steps (1 Peter 2:21; 1 John 2:6).

There is much social distress in various areas but, as a leading preacher has aptly said, "We have sometimes been slow to implement our convictions with joint vigorous social action." Though we can each, in our small corners, emulate the Merciful One, there are great things we can and should do together.

True, we try to help the socially distressed—the aged, the handicapped, the mentally disabled—but there is still so much to be done. We extend the arm of mercy to mentally ill children, of which there are a surprisingly large number. Jesus helped such children, too, for we learn that the Syrophoenician woman's daughter, whom Jesus healed, was one of these.

A Heathen Culture

This woman of Syrophoenicia suffered continual anguish because of the horribly strange malady of her little daughter. In desperation she went to Jesus, and He helped her and proclaimed her, a heathen woman, a heroine of faith. Many women were ardent followers of Jesus during His earthly ministry, but He said only of this one distressed mother, "Woman, great is thy faith" (Matt. 15:28).

Matthew calls her a woman of Canaan. She was of ancient Semitic extraction—of a people cursed almost to extinction because of sensual and barbarous idolatry.

The Israelites, under Joshua, had driven the Canaanites out of the land, but Asher, whose portion of land extended to the northern boundary, did not drive out the enemy. The Canaanites that remained had settled in the north and had occupied a narrow strip of land, some twenty miles long and from two to forty-five miles wide, along the Mediterranean Sea.

Weak in agriculture, not large enough to be a military power, protected by the sea to the west and the mountains to the east, they had become a notable industrial and commercial nation, which became known as Phoenicia. The Phoenicians excelled in shipbuilding; they had the only great navy in the world and held the monopoly on the shipping trade. They were world-famous for their metalwork and exceptionally fine glassware. Some of their delicately beautiful glass vases are on display in our large art museums.

We learn from the Old Testament prophets that Phoenicia was a notable and wealthy power. Historians agree that Ezekiel, in chapters 26 to 28, gives a priceless description of the greatness and beauty of Phoenicia with its great cities—among them Tyre, the most splendid city in the world at that time, beautiful in situation with its busy harbor crowded with majestic ships. Even when Jesus lived its principal cities were more populous and important than Jerusalem.

Though heathen, the people were intensely religious, serving many gods. Living so close to the Jewish people, intermingling (1 Kings 16:31) often on friendly terms (1 Kings 9:11–14; 26–28), they named their gods after the attributes of the great Jehovah (for example, their gods' names meant the great, the strong, the supreme, my lord).

Mark tells us that the woman of Canaan was Syrophoenician by race—the Phoenicians having merged with Syria. Later, the little country was taken over by the Greeks, and consequently, by culture and language she was a Greek. The Greek is also identified with Gentile (see Rom. 1:16).

A Great Need in a Dark Corner

This poor woman, living in a spiritually dark corner of the earth, naturally believed that her child was demon-possessed, for she had likely called on many healers and used every medicine available, yet her daughter was "grievously vexed." What grief tore at her heart when her little girl was thrown into violent paroxysms and there was nothing she could do to bring relief. She grew desperate and weary with anxiety and the constant care of her child.

Then one day she heard of Jesus, and a new hope began to push away the darkness of despair. There was a rumor that Jehovah had visited the Jewish people by sending a great prophet—an unusual prophet—who healed all kinds of diseases. She also heard that people from Tyre and Sidon had gone down to distant Galilee (Luke 6:17) and had actually been healed by this great Jewish physician. No doubt she inquired about Him—where He was, how He healed—and she was told that some had only to touch Him, for even His robe diffused healing power!

The more she heard about Him the more excited she became. Would He help her too? She must find Him! When she heard that Jesus was approaching the borders of her own country, she started out to find Him with new courage and a faith based on stories she had heard of His marvelous power to heal the deaf, dumb, and blind. Best of all was the latest news, that in Gadara the Prophet-Physician had expelled legions of devils from a man (Luke 8:26–40).

The Syrophoenician woman did not have to travel far to find Jesus. Perhaps He had come to the borderland to avoid the Pharisees, who were no doubt angry, for He had openly exposed them (Matt. 15:1–7). Surely He had come to rest and relax because He wished for seclusion (Mark 7:24). Jesus never rushed though He had much to do. He never let business push prayer out of His life, as we so often do. Though His was a great world-shaking mission, and He had only a brief three years to accomplish it, He often took time for rest, quiet, and prayer.

A Great Plea in a Dark Corner

Jesus could not be hid, for men were always drawn to Him. As soon as the woman of Canaan saw Jesus she was certain that it was He. She called out, "Have mercy on me, O Lord, thou Son of David; my daughter is grievously vexed with a devil" (Matt. 15:22).

Though she did not realize it, the core of the gospel was in her respectful address. What marvelous words to come from heathen lips, "O Lord, thou Son of David." How utterly earnest, heartrending, and humble her prayer. What great mother-love that made spiritual and physical distress of her daughter her own overwhelming burden!

How shall we explain the apparent unconcern of Jesus, the Merciful One? He did not even answer her impassioned pleadings but turned from her and went into the house. Had he come some fifty miles on foot through mountainous country and over rugged roads to save a lost sheep or to turn it into the dark night of sinful environment? Perhaps he had a greater design than to heal a sick body. Could it be to try her faith, to teach her perseverance in prayer? That He surely accomplished, for she cried all the more entreatingly: "Have mercy . . . have mercy . . ."

The disciples, annoyed by the Syrophoenician woman's loud cries, may have said, "Send this dog of a heathen away. She is making such a commotion that everyone will come running and You, Master, will get no rest." But neither the inconsiderate conduct of the disciples nor the silence of Jesus could drive the woman away, and she cried out all the more. When Jesus finally answered her He said, "I am not sent but unto the lost sheep of the house of Israel" (Matt. 15:24). His apparent reproach only drove her to deeper humility. Falling sorrowfully and reverently at His feet, she became a beggar for grace. Her whole soul became entreaty and, with urgency, she pleaded, "Lord, help me."

When Jesus replied to her piteous plea (Matt. 15:26) she was quick to turn the seeming slight into an argument. Disclaiming the privileges of a child of Israel, she begged for the crumbs of mercy that fell from the table of His chosen people. Like the little dogs that ate the crumbs the children dropped, she would be thankful for little mercies.

A Great Faith in a Dark Corner

Step by step this burdened mother was tried. But by her great need, her strength of will, astonishing earnestness, great humility, and vigorous faith she held on, and, like Jacob with the angel, she persevered until Jesus gave the coveted blessing. The disciples could never forget this compelling scene nor the admiration in the voice of Jesus when He said, "Woman, great is thy faith: be it unto thee even as thou wilt" (Matt. 15:28). Jesus did not give her the crumbs but the children's bread. Her resolute faith was rewarded and her daughter was healed. Even though Jesus had first sent His disciples to the lost sheep of the house of Israel (Matt. 10:5–6), they learned in this house on the border of a heathen land that Jesus does not hear and save on the basis of kinship with Abraham but on the basis of faith. They understood Jesus when later in His ministry He said, "Other sheep I have, which are not of this fold" (John 10:16).

A woman with such a vigorous faith, the humble recipient of great blessings, without a doubt joined the host of others who could not keep silent but published throughout the whole city and land how such great things Jesus had done (Luke 8:39). Her grateful theme must have been, "He hath done all things well" (Mark 7:37).

Could this woman of Syrophoenicia have been a charter member of the church at Tyre? We read in Acts 21:2–6 that some years later Paul and his companion spent a week in Tyre with the community of believers there. Was this heroine of faith one of those who knelt on the sands of the Mediterranean beach to pray that God would bless and prosper the missionary to the Gentiles?

The story of the Syrophoenician woman is a shining example to all mothers. Her perseverance in prayer was truly wonderful, her humility equally so, and her faith in His power was outstanding. Our daughters, too, are in need of prevailing prayer, for they are often the victims of evil influence, pride, selfishness, and wayward-ness. God only knows what wonders could be done if we prayed for our daughters as the Syrophoenician woman prayed for hers.

Suggestions for Discussion

1. Of whom were the Canaanites descendants (Gen. 9:26; 10:6, 15 –18)?
2. What did Jesus say about Tyre and Sidon (Matt. 11:20 –24)?
3. How and where do we as a church group care for handicapped children? Why should we support these institutions?
4. Did Jesus really cast devils out of people, or was that just the way these ancient people referred to strange diseases (e.g., Mark 3; Luke 4:41; 8:35; and so on)?
5. A great philosopher once said that parents love their children more than children love their parents. Do you agree?
6. How do you account for this heathen woman calling Jesus the Son of David? What does this title mean? What other vital concepts of salvation are found in her address and prayer?
7. Explain Jesus' attitude toward this woman.
8. Did Jesus teach persistence in prayer on any other occasion?
9. It appears to have been rather common for a Jew to call a Gentile a dog. What is the relationship between Jews and Christians today?
10. Is there as much power in prayer now as in Jesus' day? Do we hear about children being healed because of the prayers of parents?
11. Jesus said, "Woman, great is thy faith." What kind of faith did this woman have?

But many that are first shall be last; and the last shall be first.
—Matthew 19:30

24

Salome

Scripture Reading
Matthew 20:20–28; 27:55–56;
Mark 15:40–41; 16:14

America is the land of opportunity for everyone. Though some people are discriminated against, they also have their champions. After a time—it may be a rather long time—we believe that America will be the land of equal opportunity for all. Great things can be done in America by those from humble beginnings. That is one of the things that is so wonderful about the American way of life.

There is, however, a popular spirit in America that is basically selfish. It is the spirit of *you first after me.* I believe in myself and, competitively speaking, the prize is to the one that gets there first.

If Christian people who adopt the *first come, first served* standard would seriously read and ponder the philosophy of Jesus, they would learn that the attitude of *me first* is exactly opposite to the teachings of the Living Word.

It is assumed by many that we need political influence to get somewhere in life. We need to know someone who will give us a boost (but keep this confidential, you know) up the ladder of success. Salome, the mother of John and James, thought she knew the way to success when she tried to use her influence with Jesus to get high positions for her sons in the kingdom. Salome was ashamed when Jesus explained that the way to success is to place God first, others second, and ourselves last.

What a revolution the application of this teaching of Jesus would make in America, in our personal lives, in our homes, and even in our churches!

Salome Is Generous

Salome was one of the more prominent of the group of notable women who ministered to Jesus. She is not mentioned with the original few women (Luke 8:2–3) who gave of their substance in the first year of His ministry. It seems that she joined them later when she was free to leave her home and devote herself to full-time service for Jesus.

In Mark she is called Salome (Mark 15:40; 16:1), but Matthew calls her the mother of Zebedee's children (Matt. 20:20; 27:56). Matthew wrote at a later date than Mark, and by that time Zebedee may have died. Perhaps her son James was already in glory, and John had gained prominence as a great apostle and author. So Matthew thinks of her, not so much for her own worthiness, or as the wife of a prosperous man, but as the mother of James and John.

When we first read about Salome she had been married for many years, for she had two grown sons. Her husband, Zebedee, was a fisherman on the Sea of Galilee (Matt. 4:21). He owned boats, nets, and all the necessary equipment for his occupation. His sons, James and John, worked with him, and there is evidence that Peter and Andrew were partners with Zebedee and his sons (Luke 5:1–11). They had a prosperous business catching and selling fish. When we learn that John was a friend of the High Priest, we presume that they had business dealings together. The fact that Zebedee had others in his employ (Mark 1:20) would indicate that he was a wealthy businessman and, consequently, belonged to the upper middle class of his day. We know that Salome was a woman of means and social position for she had both the wealth to provide for the needs of Jesus and the time to follow Him about.

Salome was deeply interested in the kingdom that Jesus had come to establish and was a generous contributor to His cause. Could it be that Salome and Zebedee also provided Jesus with a home in Capernaum? By his own admission Jesus owned nothing, not even a "place to lay His head," yet He spent so much time in Capernaum that it came to be called His own city (Matt. 4:13; 9:1; 17:25; Mark 2:1; John 6:24).

Salome was the sister of the Virgin Mary. Though all do not agree that she was, a comparison of Matthew 27:55–56 and John 19:25 makes this relationship quite certain. That made Jesus Salome's nephew, John and James His cousins, and it was Uncle Zebedee who owned the big fishing business. This relationship may be a reason for bringing His family, friends, and widowed mother to Capernaum (John 2:12).

Capernaum, where Salome likely lived, was on the north shore of Lake Galilee near Bethsaida, which was the town of Andrew, Peter, and Philip. One day, when Jesus was walking along the shore between Bethsaida and Capernaum, He saw Andrew and Peter mending nets, and John and James working in the boat. He called all four to be His disciples (Matt. 4:18–22). Because they left their work at a moment's notice, Zebedee was shorthanded, but he did not complain. Somehow he knew that James and John were being called to a higher service. Salome, too, was generous with more than money— she willingly gave her two wonderful sons to Jesus, and, because of this, she will be honored forever.

Interested

Salome was a good woman, a reverent and faithful daughter of Israel. She was one of the few who still looked for the consolation of Israel. She did not object when John left home to attend the preaching of John the Baptist in the wilderness. John was captivated by the powerful spirit-filled preacher and became his disciple. When John came home to Salome with the exciting report of the Baptist's new gospel, she believed that he was a great prophet.

There in the wilderness, John had been introduced to the Lamb of God and had visited with Him, followed Him into Galilee, and had never been the same since. John and James had been irresistibly drawn to Jesus as they listened to the profound things He said and saw the manifestations of His supernatural power. Though they went back to their home and fishing nets, their hearts belonged to Jesus. And Salome understood, for she began to ponder the things her son told her about Jesus and to earnestly recall God's promises, and came to believe that Jesus was the One who should come—the Messiah. Her understanding and consent no doubt strengthened and increased the faith of her sons in the Lord Jesus.

Ambitious

Salome had unusually gifted sons, and so we assume that she was an intelligent woman. However, because she did not understand the true nature of Jesus' kingdom, she made a stupid mistake. She was not the only one who did not understand that His was a spiritual kingdom. She was only sharing the views of all the disciples (John 1:49; 6:15). Not even John, the closest of all to Jesus, understood that when He spoke of His death (Matt. 20:17–22), His kingdom was not of this world.

The question of greatness in the kingdom often vexed the disciples, and Jesus had to teach them many a lesson in humility (Matt. 18:1– 4). But until the very last they still expected the kingdom of Jesus to be a visible and political one. Even when they were eating the bread and drinking the cup of the New Testament, and while Judas slunk out of the door of the Upper Room to betray the Master, they got into a violent argument as to which of them would have the best position in the new regime (Luke 22:24–30).

There was keen competition among the disciples. The beloved John and loyal James were as eager as the rest, and Salome knew all about it. Perhaps Salome's sons were a bit worried that the position of greatest honor would go to Peter, for Jesus, who was intimate with him, only a few days before had been answering Peter's question when He promised thrones to the disciples (Matt. 19:27–28).

Mother Salome was proud of her gifted, stalwart sons and was ambitious for them. "Just leave it to me, my boys," we can imagine she said. "No one will lord it over you, no, not even Peter, the rock! I have influence with Jesus if anyone has! Does Peter's mother follow Him about or has Philip's mother given Him a home? Besides, His mother is my sister—that should mean a thing or two! Yes, I will settle this squabbling once and for all. You, my two sons, will sit high above the others." And Salome determined to have a talk with Jesus without delay.

As Jesus was making His last journey to Jerusalem, Salome was in the crowd that followed Him. It was the beginning of the last week of His life, and He was in the vicinity of Jericho when Salome detached herself from the crowd and came before Jesus. Though ambitious and sure of herself, Salome was tactful as she made her daring request in the presence of so many people. She looked humble as she bowed low at the feet of the King of the Jews, but her heart was not humble. It was full of pride, presumption, and selfishness. She had no concern for the hurt feelings, jealousy, and bitterness (Matt. 20:24) that would surely ensue if both her sons were favored.

How different the selfish, conceited prayer of Salome was from the prayer of the humble Syrophoenician woman who had bowed low before the Lord! Did Jesus think of that as He quietly rebuked her, "Salome, you know not what you ask"? Looking at her sons beside her He asked, "Are you able to drink of my cup?" John and James, uncomprehending but confident, replied, "We are able!" Gravely the Master said, "You shall indeed. . . ."

The prophetic words of Jesus were all but lost in the explosion of chagrin and anger all around Him. Jesus quickly quieted the disciples (Matt. 20:25) and then went on to give His famous definition of true greatness, "Whosoever will be great among you, let him be your minister; and whosoever will be chief among you, let him be your servant" (Matt. 20:26–27).

Salome's request was denied, but it was honored in that her son James would be the first to attain immortality as a martyr (Acts 12:2) and John the last disciple to suffer for the glory of the Cross (Rev. 1:9).

Loyal

With many people looking on, Salome was taught a much-needed lesson in humility. She learned that greatness comes in proportion to self-giving. Because of her record of service for Jesus, her social position, and the self-confidence that comes with wealth, she could have turned away with hurt pride, but Salome learned her lesson for she remained a loyal follower of Jesus to the end.

She followed her Lord to Calvary. When every disciple but John had run from the scene of the Crucifixion in terror and confusion, Salome stood near the cross with John and the mother of Jesus. Hostile, mocking faces gleamed in the darkness all around them, but they would not leave the One they loved, even though that loyalty might involve personal danger.

Salome listened as Jesus commended His mother to John, and we think that Salome shared this holy duty and honor with her son. With sorrowing Mary between them, they comforted one another as they went back to John's home in the city.

Salome had seen her Savior die and, with the same devotion, went to the grave to lavishly anoint His dead body with preservative spices (Mark 16:1–8).

Because Salome was loyal, loving, and generous to the very end, she had an intimate acquaintanceship with the Son of David, His honored disciples, and personal friends. She saw the awful death of the world's Redeemer and, with her own ears, heard the incredible but triumphant words of God's angel, "He is risen!"

Suggestions for Discussion

1. How would it work out if in society, church, and family life Christian people would do as Paul advised in Romans 12:10?

2. What does Jesus say about those who want to be important? See Matthew 19:30.

3. How did Salome show her generosity? Does generosity always have its reward?

4. If Salome was a sister to the Virgin Mary, what relation was she to Elisabeth? In view of this relationship, how much previous knowledge could John and James have had about John the Baptist? About Jesus?

5. What did Jesus often talk about and what incidents occurred that helped to build up hope for a new regime in the minds of His followers?

6. Why was it so difficult for Jesus' friends and disciples to comprehend many of His teachings?

7. What is amazing about Salome's request of Jesus?

8. Was this request all Salome's idea? See Mark 10:35–45.

9. Was it only arrogance on the part of James and John, or did they possess qualifications for greatness? If so, what were they?

10. Was there anything commendable in Salome's request?

11. What builds a stronger character: success through work and struggle or success with the help (financial or otherwise) of parents?

12. May we, or should we, pray for great honors for our children?

13. How can greatness be achieved through humility?

14. What unusual experiences did Salome have?

15. Now that you have studied Salome, what do you think of her?

*Come, see a man, which told me all things that ever
I did: is not this the Christ?*
—John 4:29

25

The Samaritan Woman

Scripture Reading
John 4:1–42

$\mathscr{W}$hen John tells the story of the woman of Samaria, he pictures one of the greatest scenes in the Bible. He repeats the conversation between Jesus and the woman with an artistry and finesse that portrays the feelings of the woman and the compelling power of Jesus. It is a dramatic story, and it is told so vividly that we could easily believe John had been at the well himself, quietly listening and intently watching. Only John tells us about this day in the life of our Lord and of the conversation freighted with meaning for all people—yet every day in our Lord's life must have been as full and fruitful as this day.

It is high noon, and the Master is weary. His feet are hot and tired, and His clothes smell like the dust of the Samaritan road. It is a very human young man who slumps exhausted to the well curb.

He is hungry and thirsty. He peers longingly into the deep well, but He has no bucket to draw the water up. Perhaps the disciples will bring a bucket from Sychar where they have gone to buy food.

Jesus had come a long way on foot that morning. Both He and John the Baptist had been preaching and baptizing in Judea. After John had said of Jesus, "Behold the Lamb of God . . . He is preferred before me . . . ," people began to flock to Jesus in great numbers. The Jewish spiritual leaders disliked John but hated Jesus more for His still greater popularity, and they tried desperately to turn popular opinion against both John and Jesus. When Jesus heard of the interference of the Pharisees, He left Judea to avoid any trouble that might arise from the apparent rivalry between Himself and John.

He chose to go through Samaria to Galilee. The Jews and Samaritans hated each other, and most Jews preferred to go around Samaria (even if it meant crossing the Jordan twice) rather than meet a Samaritan in his own land. His disciples must have wondered why He deliberately chose to go through that area. He would have to stop en route—where was His Jewish spirit? They did not yet realize that He knew all things and that He was developing His mission every day and every hour, showing Himself to the world. They also did not realize that He was revealing His purpose to His disciples and, thus, training them to be channels of spiritual blessing to people of every race, creed, and color.

The Woman

At the same time that Jesus, footsore and parched from the burning eastern sun, walked toward the well, a poor, disreputable woman from Sychar found that it was time to refill her water jar. This woman had once been beautiful but, after a life of wantonness, her pretty face was hard and bold, her once attractive figure old and weary. After a quick glance to the street, she carelessly adjusted her loose headdress over her straggling hair, tied the sash on her faded old cotton dress, picked up her water pot, and took the worn path alone to the communal well.

It could actually be enjoyable to go to the well together with other women and maidens (1 Sam. 9:11) in the early morning hours or in the evening when the valley cooled under the huge shadows of Mount Ebal and Mount Gerizim. The women and maidens exchanged pleasant, homey gossip, laughed, and even sang as they sauntered together to the well and met around its stony brim at the close of day. Once she had been one of them, but long ago their footsteps hurried from her on the hard baked path. One and then another had given her a disdainful glance and turned away from her, and she knew she was not wanted—that she was not good enough, that they despised her—for she was an adulteress! As the years went by she had been more and more alone. She chose to go to the well at midday when the sun blazed in the yellow sky and the heat waves danced on the hard path, burning through her shabby sandals. Even that was pleasant and much preferred to the smoldering resentment and superior glances of her neighbors.

Because she needed to walk alone at midday, she met the One who changed her life completely, the only One who could raise her status to respectability and beyond that, to usefulness and honor.

She did not know all this, but Jesus knew. He knew all about her sinful life. He knew how convivially she had chased pleasure and how each time, like a cheerful butterfly, it had eluded her eager fingers. He knew all about her sins and failures, her disillusionment and heartaches. Everyone knew of her evil past and her sordid present. Everyone thought that she was content to be an outcast. No one knew but Jesus, who was watching her approach from His seat in the shade at the well, that she hated herself and her sordid life, that she wanted to be different—respectable. Her neighbors would have snickered into their scarves if she had ever told them she really didn't want to be what she was.

She was dissatisfied and bitter as she sauntered to the well. Grimly she looked the other way when she saw that the dusty young man on the well curb was a Jew. When the fatigued young man said, "Give me a drink," she sharply retorted, "How is it that *you* ask *me* for a drink? I know as well as you what you Jews think of us, the

Samaritans. You think that you are far above us—not that I agree. Is it not beneath your dignity to ask a favor of me?"

Jesus knew all about the ancient feud, of the hate that never died between the Jews and the Samaritans. He looked from heaven ages ago to seek the wicked ten tribes of Israel deported by the Assyrians. He knew how the inhabitants of Israel were replaced by foreigners (2 Kings 17:24) who intermarried with those left of Israel, and how they copied the worship of God, adding to it their own idolatry. He knew the whole sordid history of the people of Israel and Samaria, and His holy anger had burned against their sensuous, senseless idolatry. Now, as He looked from the foot of Mount Gerizim to the temple on its bulky top, did He think again of the unholy competition between those who worshiped at the temple in Jerusalem and those who worshiped at the one on Mount Gerizim? Did he think of the people's stubborn pride and contempt for each other?

The Well

Ignoring the sarcasm and the allusion to the ancient dispute, He said, "I know your need, your desire for a better life—I can give it to you as a gift. It is living water! But you must ask Me for it."

"It sounds interesting," said the woman, "but aren't You rather presumptuous?" Mocking, she said, "You surely are an arrogant Jew if You think You are greater than our father Jacob who dug this well and used it himself." The pride and the confidence of the Jew was in Abraham (John 8:33, 39), but the Samaritans boasted with as much gusto about father Jacob who had lived in the valley between the mountains of Gerizim and Ebal (Deut. 11:29; Josh. 8:32–35). Jacob had raised his large family and built his altars in the long shadows of great Gerizim until Dinah had occasioned the shameful act against the Shechemites (Gen. 34–35:1). Jacob's well remained a hallowed spot, the feet of thirsty ones had worn grooves in the stony steps, and shepherds watering their flocks had turned the windlass for many centuries.

Jesus ignored the scorn. His discerning eye saw a thirsty soul, and He said, "The water I have for you will make your life over. It will blot out your sordid past. It will cleanse you and make you perfectly whole. It will give you peace, the favor of God, and an inner beauty that will grow into eternity."

She was perplexed, but in her heart there was a thirst for something higher and better when she said, "Give me this living water." Jesus said, "I will, but you must first confess your sin."

When Jesus said, "Call thy husband," He was not changing the subject but was compelling her to face her sin. In a flash, her sinful past and present life stood like a bold, ugly specter in the presence of the sinless one. Her defiant shoulders drooped, her jeering tone turned to one low with shame, as she said, "I have no husband." She was alone with Jesus when He reproved her and laid bare all the guilty secrets of her depraved life. With marvelous tact He put emphasis, not on the bad in her, but on the one good thing He saw in her. He said, "You have been truthful." Who ever paid her a compliment? Surely not the man who lived with her but did not respect her enough to marry her. No one thought she had *any* moral integrity.

She exclaimed, "You must be—yes, You are a prophet! You can help me in my search for truth! Tell me—where must I worship, and why, and how?"

"God is a Spirit: and they that worship him must worship him in spirit and in truth" (John 4:24). With these wonderful words of Jesus the whole burden of dispute and tradition was forever removed and made of no importance.

Marveling, the woman said, "God is a Spirit? What do you mean? Then I can worship God anywhere? That is a new idea!" Under the spell of the Great Prophet she softly shared her secret hope, "I know positively that when the Messiah comes He will tell us all things!"

Jesus replied, "I am He, the one speaking to you." In a flash the startled woman knew why she had been so moved in His presence, and she believed in Jesus with all her heart.

Amazing grace and revelation! When for the first time Jesus revealed His identity, it was not to the Jews, the learned, the leaders, or even the pious, but to a person of no account in the eyes of the world—to this depraved woman of a despised people. She did not demand, like the Jews, "If thou be the Christ, tell us plainly" (John 10:24), but contritely and sincerely she asked of Him and He gave her living water.

At this moment the disciples, returning from Sychar with food, interrupted the conversation as they walked up, saying, "Here is food, Master, let's eat!" How astonished they were to see Jesus and the shabby Samaritan woman talking together so earnestly. But the rapture in her face and a heavenly joy in the Savior's silenced their questions, and they waited for Jesus to give them an explanation (John 4:31–38).

The Witness

Forgetting she was thirsty, the woman hurried home. In her ardor she even forgot her precious water pot! She forgot that she was shamed and despised and poor. She had made an amazing discovery—she had met the Messiah and He had changed her life completely! Like everyone with true faith, she walked in newness of life and made haste to tell others about Jesus.

In no time she was back in the city, joyous and eager to share the good news. Her people could see that her life had been changed since Jesus came into her heart, and they believed her when she said, "Come, see . . . the Christ." When Jesus saw the people coming across the lush meadows and green corn fields of Samaria, He said to His disciples, "Lift up your eyes, and look on the fields; for they are white already to harvest" (John 4:35). And when these spiritually hungry people listened to His words they believed in Him and said, "This is indeed the Christ, the Saviour of the world" (John 4:42).

The woman of Samaria did not have a Christian home environment, and her meager knowledge of the truth was fused with pagan practices. She had wasted her life in immorality. She was despised even by her own confused countrymen. She found Jesus late in her wasted life, but she joyously stepped through heaven's portals into eternity with her arms full of sheaves. Shall we who walk in the glow of the gospel light "come rejoicing, bringing in the sheaves?"

Suggestions for Discussion

1. What events had transpired in the ministry of Jesus prior to His meeting with the woman of Samaria?
2. Was Jesus' visit in Samaria inconsistent with Matthew 10:5?
3. What made the Jews and the Samaritans so bitter toward each other (e.g., 2 Kings 17:6, 24–41; Ezra 4; Neh. 4; Mic. 1:5–9)?
4. Was Jesus actually fatigued, or did He create this occasion in order to meet the woman?
5. What is living water?
6. What kind of a person was this woman of Samaria? Was there anything attractive about her personality?
7. Was she a seeking soul, or was she drawn to Jesus almost against her will?
8. Is there something commendable about everybody?
9. When was the first time that Jesus told the Jews plainly who He was (Matt. 26:64; John 17:3)?
10. Do we have a record of later missionary work in Samaria? Was it successful? Who were the mission workers (Acts 8:5–25)?
11. What approach or methods for soul winning can we learn from the story of the Samaritan woman?

Now there stood by the cross of Jesus . . . Mary Magdalene.
—John 19:25

26

Mary Magdalene

Scripture Reading
Matthew 27:55–61; 28:1; Mark 15:40–47; 16:1–11;
Luke 8:2; 23:55–56; 24:1–11; John 19:25; 20:1–18

John, the author of the fourth gospel, was Jesus' best friend during His earthly ministry. He was one of the inner circle that formed—with great loyalty and fervent belief—around the Master. Peter, impetuous and loving, John, and his dauntless brother James, were often singled out from among the twelve disciples to witness special manifestations of the power and glory of the God-man. But of the three, John was the most intimate friend Jesus had. In his writings, John always alludes to himself as the disciple whom Jesus loved (John 19:26; 21:7).

Unlike Luke (Luke 1:1–4), John actually saw the things Jesus did and heard the gracious words of life from His own lips (John 1:14; 19:35). John had a great, lofty, and intuitive mind and was so constantly with the Master that he was saturated with His teachings. He sometimes gives us a glimpse into the very soul and mind of Jesus (John 6:5–6).

The disciples, except for Judas Iscariot, were a closely-knit group. From John's writings we learn that he was intimate with their feelings and was aware of their views (John 2:11, 21–22; 6:19; 12:16) and of what they said to one another (John 4:27, 33; 6:60–71). John also knew the women who followed Jesus and were His personal friends. Among these women, Mary Magdalene, next to the mother of Jesus, stands out the most prominently. Out of the nine times she is mentioned with the other women she is named first, with only one exception (John 19:25). John knew her very well, for they had gone through many trying, as well as exhilarating, experiences together. He admired her courage and honored her for the high place she had in the Master's esteem. John mentions her alone and by name four times in his account of the Resurrection and, thus, makes her the leading character in this crowning event. The distinction of being the first one to see the risen and glorified Lord was given, not to the disciple who Jesus loved, but to a woman who had so much to be thankful for that she could not forget nor ever leave her Lord.

Mary Magdalene's Identity

The life of Mary Magdalene is a most vivid example of what Jesus can do for a human soul. Her story begins with the darkest of all human misery and ends with the most glorious day in the history of the world.

Mary's home was in Magdala, a small town on the western shore of the Sea of Galilee. There were several Marys among Jesus' followers. She was called Mary Magdalene to distinguish her from the others. They were Mary the wife of Cleopas, Mary the sister of Martha, Mary the mother of Mark, and Mary the mother of Jesus. An ugly stigma has been attached to her name from earliest times when she became known as the reclaimed courtesan, or the fallen woman redeemed to sainthood. This is due to the unfair identification of Mary with the sinful woman who anointed the feet of Jesus in Simon's house (Luke 7:36–50).

The Roman Catholic church perpetuated this infamy by building Magdalen houses for fallen women. Some contend that art has often made her reputation by depicting Mary on canvas as an immoral woman, more voluptuous than penitent. It is doubtful that the stigma will ever be removed from her fair name. Even the dictionary defines the name Magdalene as "a reformed prostitute," because she has been traditionally identified with the woman in Simon's house. Some have added to the confusion by claiming that Mary of Bethany, the woman who was a sinner (Luke 7), and Mary Magdalene are all one person. Surely, Mary of Magdala cannot be Mary of Bethany for the gospel writers have distinguished each Mary by locality or family. Their characters were distinctly different. Mary from Bethany was quiet and meditative, while Mary of Magdala was enthusiastic and aggressive. She was the inspiring spirit among her women companions.

Three touching incidents of sinful women are recorded in the gospel—the woman of Samaria (John 4), the woman who was a sinner (Luke 7:37), and the woman taken in adultery (John 8:3–11). In none of these instances are these women mentioned by name, but Mary Magdalene's name is given repeatedly and always with distinction. To further vindicate Mary's name we might add that Jesus avoided all basis for scandal, and the Pharisees, though expert faultfinders, never accused Jesus of having a bad woman in His company.

⚜ ⚜ ⚜

What do the Scriptures say about Mary? Luke 8:2–3 says that the women who followed Jesus on His preaching tours to minister to His needs were women who had been healed of infirmities and evil spirits. Mary Magdalene was released from the torture of seven devils (also see Mark 16:9). She was not vexed as the daughter of the Syrophoenician woman was, but she was completely controlled by demons.

Demon possession was prevalent in Jesus' day, especially in the area of Gadara, which was not far from Magdala. It seemed that all the forces of hell were let loose to raise havoc where the Redeemer of the world walked on earth. There was uncontrolled hate and evil in the human heart. Satan personally did his utmost to turn Jesus aside from His purpose, and his legions entered into many people to drive them into illness, paroxysms, and insanity.

Mary's condition may have been much like that of the naked, crazed men of Gadara who lived in the tombs. They were so fierce that they tore off their iron chains and terrifed the countryside. So, we can picture Mary of Magdala bereft of will and reason, with matted hair and vacant eyes, screaming and tearing at her clothes.

Jesus had found her, perhaps in Magdala, not far from Capernaum where He lived, and He had pity on her. He had snatched her from the tombs of despair and living death. In a moment He had made her a well woman. Immediately after her restoration to normalcy and health, Mary became an ardent and active follower of Jesus. She gave generously of her wealth to supply the everyday needs of Jesus and the Twelve.

Mary's Loving Heart

Mary, perhaps thirty years of age, is thought to have been beautiful and gracious. Her love was warm and glowing. She was always enthusiastic and was scarcely able to tear herself away from the active ministry of love and kindness. She became as passionately thankful as once she had been desperately ill.

She was happiest in the Lord's company, walking in the gospel light, marveling at the miracles, feeling the pulse of the multitudes, and pitying the sheep without a shepherd. Conscious of satanic animosities, she walked proudly and unafraid with her Lord.

Mary had been aghast at Salome's request for honor on their last journey together from Galilee to Jerusalem (Matt. 20:20). All Mary wanted was to be near Jesus, for she loved Him. There was nothing she would not do for Him. He had done so much for her that she wanted to give every moment of her redeemed life to serve Him. At the end of the journey, she walked with her Lord into Jerusalem where the Lamb of God was to be made an offering for sin.

⁊ᶄ   ⁊ᶄ   ⁊ᶄ

She shared John's love and adoration for the Master. Was Mary with John in the palace of the High Priest, tensely watching the meek and lowly One suffering the indignities of a sham trial? Did her heart cry "no" at the injustice of every accusation—of sedition, of being a seducer and an enemy of the Law, of false claims to equality with God and to kingship? Was her loving heart racked when the witnesses signed the death warrant and Pilate announced the place of execution?

Mary's unstinted and unusual loyalty knew no bounds. Even though all but one of the disciples had hidden in terror, she and the other women followed the cross with the hissing mob through the appointed gate to Golgotha. There, in the fringe of the crowd, the women huddled, shaking with quiet sobs (Matt. 27:55–56). They cringed at each hammer blow, and as the cross lodged with a thud in the ground, Mary and two of the women edged among the soldiers and mockers to the foot of the cross. Her spirit and her love for Jesus were so strong that she could better stand to see His anguish than to be separated from Him.

Mary saw everything—the soldiers with their high helmets and heavy spears, joking as they cast lots for the Savior's robe—the leers and jibes. She shuddered when the tortured thieves mocked Him from their places on the conspicuous hill of death (Matt. 27:41–44).

When the Savior dismissed his mother (John 19:26–27), He kept Mary. He did not dismiss her, nor would she go away. She was not afraid in the darkness for she was near to the Lord of her life. His every word was indelibly written on her heart. He bowed His head. She saw Him die, but she would not leave even His dead body.

While Joseph of Arimathea went to ask Pilate for permission to take down the body of Jesus and Nicodemus went to buy spices, Mary waited by the cross. She stayed there until the last taunt died away on the highway by the hill (Matt. 27:39), and then she assisted Joseph and Nicodemus as they gently took down the cross and released and washed the bloody body of the Savior.

Sadly, she followed them to the grave and watched intently as the men laid Jesus on a bed of spices. She likely helped wrap His body in clean linen. This all had to be done rather hastily for there were only about three hours left before the Sabbath. Mary was not quite satisfied and resolved to come herself after the Sabbath to finish the task. After the men maneuvered the unwieldy stone to the opening of the grave, they went home. Mary, so dependent on Jesus—perhaps even fearful without Him—stayed sitting beside the tomb (Matt. 27:61).

Mary kept the Sabbath that followed, but it was filled with thoughts and tears. Over and over the awful trial and crucifixion repeated in her mind; she agonized and wept for the inhuman cruelty and injustice of it. All day long she recalled every precious word He had spoken, how His life had always been lived for others.

She loved Jesus as a person. Jesus meant everything to her. Life was not worth living without Him. She loved Him for the peace and happiness He had brought into her life, for the beauty of His perfect goodness and righteousness, for His tenderness and mercy.

Not for a moment could she forget Jesus, and early the next morning, while it was still dark, she went to the tomb with a few other women. In her eagerness she hurried ahead and, as she was last at the cross and earliest at the grave, she became the first to see the empty tomb and to witness the Resurrection (Mark 16:9; John 20:1). When she saw the empty tomb, she ran to get Peter and John and came back with them. The men saw that the body was gone and ran to tell the other disciples. But Mary, disturbed that now even His precious body was spirited away, stood alone beside the grave weeping.

When once more she stooped to look in, God made a rainbow of her tears, for she saw two angels in brilliant white, and one of them said, "Woman, why weepest thou?" (John 20:13). Astonished, she turned away. And there in the garden, by the grave that could not hold its mighty prey, the resurrected Lord showed Himself to her first of all. And the first word He spoke was, "Woman."

Who can fathom the love and tenderness of Jesus when He said, "Mary." What relief, what amazement and ecstasy there must have been in Mary's response, "Master!" In her excitement, she rushed to embrace His feet as if to keep Him forever with her (John 20:17).

Why did Jesus say, "Touch me not," when, shortly after, He allowed the other women to hold His feet as they worshiped Him (Matt. 28:9)? Mary needed to learn that her love for her Master had to assume a deeper spiritual dimension, that He would be with her in a spiritual way always, even to the end of the world.

Instead, He commissioned her to be the first messenger of the resurrected Lord (John 20:17). Trembling with astonishment and joy, she hurried to bring the glorious message of hope and of the pivotal truth of Christianity to the mourning disciples (Mark 16:10).

Mary Magdalene, whose love and devotion to Jesus is unequaled, passes from view in the Gospels with the name of the risen Lord on her lips. She represents those who cannot forget what Jesus has done for them, whose hearts forever belong to the Master.

Suggestions for Discussion

1. What quality in Mary Magdalene is outstanding from the very first time she is mentioned in Scripture?
2. How is she an example to all redeemed womanhood?
3. How do we usually show our gratitude to the Lord—daily or spasmodically?
4. Explain how Mary, who once had been mentally ill, could stand the tension and strain of Calvary.
5. Describe Mary's personality.
6. What is the pivotal truth of Christianity (1 Cor. 15:17–22)?

7. What, according to the gospel writers, did the gospel do for women (Matt. 28:9–10; Mark 16:9; Luke 8:1–3; Acts 1:14; 2:18)?

Neither let us tempt Christ, as some of them also tempted, and were destroyed. . . .
—1 Corinthians 10:9

27

Sapphira

Scripture Reading
Acts 5:1–11

The promises Jesus had made to His disciples had come true (Luke 24:49). How gloriously He had fulfilled His word—and the half of it had not been told them!

In the evening of the resurrection day, Jesus had breathed on the disciples and said, "Receive ye the Holy Ghost" (John 20:22), and immediately they received the gift of spiritual insight. Understanding and believing in that mission of the Christ, they found peace. Under the power of His divine breath, they became alive to God. "As my Father hath sent me," said the ascending Lord, "even so send I you" (John 20:21). The Christian church was born, and from that hour the Eleven became so aware of their divine calling and mission that it absorbed all their waking thoughts and ambitions.

This gift of the Holy Spirit was imparted not only to the Eleven, but also to others who had gathered with them—to those who stayed together in prayer and praise and worship (Luke 24:53; Acts 1:14–15). Among them were the women who had witnessed the Resurrection. Together they recalled the teachings of Jesus, and for the first time the wondrous spiritual pattern of His ministry became clear. With the outpouring of the Spirit on Pentecost, a full understanding of the new dispensation broke on the horizon of the church.

Peter, the first spokesman of the Christian church, explained boldly and lucidly the development and fulfillment of prophecy regarding Jesus of Nazareth (Acts 2–3). He climaxed his first sermon by saying: "God hath made that same Jesus, whom ye have crucified, both Lord and Christ" (Acts 2:36). There was a tremendous response to Peter's preaching.

On that Pentecost, the despised Galileans turned the world upside down! The unusual happenings brought curious Jews from all over Jerusalem. They must have kept coming and going and saying, "An amazing thing is going on in the Upper Room. . . . Where? . . . Come and see!"

All day long there were crowds on this street—amazed, trembling, fearful, pleading. All day long Peter and the other apostles spoke from the roof in many tongues, "Repent . . . repent . . . be baptized . . . and ye shall receive the gift of the Holy Ghost" (Acts 2:38). In answer to the impassioned plea of Peter and the inspired apostles, about three thousand people passed through a unique experience that day and became the nuclei of the new church of the living God.

The names that swelled the church rolls were not of nominal members, nor did they come forward to accept Christ only to forget, the way many have at evangelistic campaigns since. They were not afraid of Jewish ecclesiastical opposition, contempt, or persecution. In spite of the unusual and sudden change in views and relationships, they persevered in the faith. "They continued steadfastly in the apostles' doctrine and fellowship, and in breaking of bread, and in prayers" (Acts 2:42).

Great wonders and signs were performed by the apostles as the Lord had predicted (Mark 16:17–18). God's power was so strikingly manifested that all the people were filled with unusual reverence, piety, and seriousness, and with unusual love and concern for one another. The early church has left us an example of unity of interests, faith, and brotherhood. That unity was vital to the preservation of the church and was the direct result of the indwelling of the Holy Spirit. Where is this united, fervent spirit today? Where do we hear the passionate cry, "What must I do to be saved?"

> Lord make my heart thine altar
> And thy love the flame!

Many generously sold their property and possessions to provide for the needy. Barnabas, because he was an outstanding Christian, a foreigner, and a talented preacher and missionary (Acts 11:22–30), is mentioned by name (Acts 4:32–37). He denied himself that he might dedicate his all to Christ. So there was great fervor and faith, great love and exemplary generosity in the early church. Filled with the Spirit, the church prospered and grew rapidly. It leaped the bounds of nationality, and the command of Jesus to bring the gospel to the ends of the earth was enthusiastically carried out (Mark 16:15).

Sapphira Holds Back

All were impressed by the example of Barnabas, among them Ananias and his wife, Sapphira. They took the words of Jesus literally: "Sell whatsoever thou hast, and give to the poor, and thou shalt have treasure in heaven" (Mark 10:21), and "whosoever he be of you that forsaketh not all that he hath, he cannot be my disciple" (Luke 14:33).

The new church was happy to have Ananias and Sapphira join them. They were a fine Christian couple. They shared their viewpoints and religious convictions; they understood and appreciated one another. Together they had left Judaism and courageously allied themselves to the cause of Jesus. They were Christian in deed as well as in name. They attended preaching and prayer meeting faithfully and were willing to sacrifice for the cause. They actually sold their property to help the needy. How many in your church would do this? How many love others that much?

Now, if this were the end of the story of Sapphira, she would have enjoyed prestige, the love of the brethren, and, in the life to come, great reward. She would have been an outstanding example of "seeking first the kingdom." But the Lord knew Sapphira better than her fellow church members did, for they looked on the outward appearance, but God looked into her heart.

Very likely Ananias and Sapphira were jealous of the prestige of Barnabas, of the praise heaped upon him by the admiring membership of the first church. Besides, they were a bit uncomfortable owning so much property when so many were parting with their possessions for the sake of Christ. Then, too, they were caught in the wave of enthusiasm that was sweeping the new church (Acts 4:32–37). They were in agreement with its principles and knew that, in this kind of community, generous giving was inescapable.

The day came when Ananias likely suggested, "I suppose we should do our share. What do you think, Sapphira? Shall we sell some of our land for the community? So many have done it now."

"What else can we do?" said Sapphira. "But if we do, let us sell it all, like Barnabas did—did you notice how pleased Peter was when Barnabas brought his gift? And, everywhere I go, all I hear about is Barnabas . . . Barnabas . . . and what a *fine* man he is. I just keep thinking about it until it irks me! Let us show the apostles that he is not the only faithful one . . . the Spirit was given to all of us! Let the people pass their praises our way for a change."

So Ananias found a buyer, and the deal was made; but when Sapphira saw the money she couldn't bear to part with all of it. She wondered how long her wardrobe would hold out, thought of the lovely materials for gowns in the Rachel Shop in the Square, of the little luxuries she would have to forego. . . .

Because we know Sapphira, we can almost hear her say, "Must we give it *all*? What if this new venture should fail? What if we do not have a farthing left—and no children either to care for us in our old age? And how I'd hate to be poor! No, Ananias, it is ideal certainly. But, after all—we must use our common sense. If we don't watch out for ourselves, who will?" Already, admiring glances were going their way. People were saying, "Did you hear about Ananias and Sapphira? Isn't that wonderful. Such love for the church! Such examples for all!"

Then Sapphira and her husband put their heads together and decided to keep a sizable amount and say, nevertheless, "Here is our all for the Master's use." Who was to know the difference? Sapphira could hardly wait to see how it would impress this one and that one. We can safely say that this was not the first time that Sapphira was dishonest in her religious life or in her relations with others.

⅔   ⅔   ⅔

It has been conjectured that Sapphira was the instigator of this whole hypocritical affair—that it was she who coveted both the praise and the money. It was with her approval and collaboration that the real estate was sold and with her consent that Ananias withheld part of the price (Acts 5:1–2). Her guilt may have been the greatest, for was she not called of God to be a helpmeet (good) for her husband, to encourage him in his service to God, to influence him for good and not evil all her days?

Sapphira knew better. She confessed to be one of those whose very way of life was founded on the principles of truth. She knew that the God of truth hated all lying lips (Ps. 101:7; Prov. 19:5). Jesus had called to the sham religionists in her own city, "Ye are of your father the devil. . . . he is a liar, and the father of it" (John 8:44). She saw the power of the Holy Spirit as it changed people from being selfish and greedy to loving and generous.

There are professing Christians among us who love money—who lie to get it and lie to keep it. The love of money is still the root of all evil and accounts for much lukewarmness in God's service. It is the real reason why the church, charities, and missions must go begging. This story is a warning to all who give dimes when they should give dollars, who cannot afford to give for a needy cause just now (for who is to know what is laid away in the safety deposit box). It is a warning to all who tell lies—little ones, bold ones, black ones, gray ones. If God swiftly punished every Ananias and Sapphira in the church today, how many do you think would be left to occupy the heavenly mansions? We do not deal with another God or a different set of principles in the twenty-first century.

Sapphira's Sad End

Ananias went to bring the gift to Peter. Three hours later Sapphira went to the assembly of the saints to see how the gift was received. Did she think that the awe on the faces of those present was admiration for her? Did she think, *Look how they notice me now?* She didn't feel quite as happy as she had anticipated—somehow the money at home in the little brown jug kept disturbing her. *Where was Ananias?* (How could she know that she would soon join him in ignominious death?)

With a pious smile she went directly to Peter for thanks and a compliment. Perhaps Peter surprised her a bit with, "Is this the entire amount for which you sold the land?" Without flinching, she said, "Yes, for so much." Peter, filled with holy anger for the honor of the Lord and with zeal for the purity of the church, pronounced a solemn and shocking sentence on Sapphira (Acts 5:9). In one ghastly moment she expired at Peter's feet, hypocrisy still on her face and unforgiven sin in her heart. She was quickly buried beside her husband with whom she had collaborated to fool herself, the church, and even the omniscient God.

And Sapphira's money was still in the little jug on the shelf. Today we often hear the glib comment about money, *You can't take it with you so why not live it up.* Do you know that you can take it with you if you *give it up?* "And Jesus answered and said, . . . There is no man that hath left house . . . or lands, for my sake, and the gospel's, but he shall receive a hundredfold now in this time . . . and in the world to come eternal life" (Mark 10:29–30).

Suggestions for Discussion

1. What differences are there between the communal state as it existed in the early church and communism? What inspired the early church to practice communal living?
2. What good things can you say about Sapphira?
3. What got her into trouble?
4. Is it better to give anonymously or openly?
5. Which is the better way to give to the church, by means of the budget or through freewill offering?
6. What does this incident teach us about the Holy Spirit?
7. Was the sin of Sapphira an unforgivable sin?
8. What makes the sin of lying so hard to detect? To correct? Are there different degrees of lying? What should children be taught about this?
9. What was the effect of Sapphira's sin and punishment on the church? What effect does it have on church members when a member is censured or excommunicated?

For as the body without the spirit is dead, so faith without works is dead also.
—James 2:26

28

$\mathcal{D}$orcas

Scripture Reading
Acts 9:36–43

$\mathcal{G}$race is the free unmerited favor of God, given in its highest degree in Jesus Christ, who came into the world to save sinners. Paul tells us, "For by grace are ye saved through faith; and that not of yourselves: it is the gift of God: not of works, lest any man should boast" (Eph. 2:8–9). Yet knowledge of our sins and miseries, or even deliverance from them, cannot alone give us a fruitful life or fulfill God's design for us.

Many who have inherited rich spiritual concepts, whose very bounds of life are fixed by good Christian principles, have a tendency to complacency. Those who sit at ease in Zion, preening denominational feathers, must rise with the energizing conviction that we are saved for a purpose. We are saved to serve God and our neighbor. Christ "gave himself for us, that he might redeem us from all iniquity, and purify unto himself a peculiar people, zealous of good works" (Titus 2:14).

How easy to sing with zest, "I am so glad that Jesus loves me," and be satisfied with a passive Christianity. How many quite comfortably ignore the fact that all who are in Christ are new creatures—and that they are known by their fruits. Jesus taught by the example of His life and by emphatic precept that "he that abideth in me, and I in him, the same bringeth forth much fruit. . . . Herein is my Father glorified, that ye bear much fruit; so shall ye be my disciples" (John 15:5, 8).

May the study of the life of Dorcas, a true disciple, awaken us from smug lethargy. The gates of heaven will not swing open for those who bask in blessings or know how to say, "Lord, Lord," but for those who, like Dorcas, have done the will of the heavenly Father. Dorcas was "full of good works and almsdeeds" (Acts 9:36).

Dorcas Was Good for Herself

After the outpouring of the Holy Spirit on Pentecost, Christians had traveled about, often impelled by persecution, and had brought the gospel of salvation through Jesus Christ everywhere. Many churches were established in Judea, Galilee, and Samaria (Acts 9:31). That there was also a church at Joppa is certain from the presence of disciples, saints, Dorcas, and hospitable Simon.

Dorcas was a compassionate and benevolent woman who was, first of all, a disciple. She had learned that to "love one another as I have loved you" found its full meaning in practice. She was a doer as well as a hearer of His Word.

Dorcas was the Greek name for the Hebrew *Tabitha,* which means gazelle—that is, beautiful, graceful. Peter called her Tabitha, but the people of Joppa called her Dorcas. As Dorcas, her name has been perpetuated in all the women's societies whose object is charity, more specifically, sewing for the poor.

This woman disciple was not important in the estimation of the world. She may not even have been as beautiful as her name suggests. She was not a Deborah or a poet like Hannah. She did not have sons to dedicate to Jesus as did Salome. She could do nothing spectacular, but she did what she could, and that is to her lasting credit. Hers was the humble but worthwhile service of the needle. Her days were spent in sewing new garments, washing and smoothing rough old cloth, and in remaking, fitting, and mending garments for the poor.

The work was tedious and required endless patience and unselfish dedication. But we know that each garment Dorcas made was stitched with threads of love, each seam was closed with kind thoughts, and each coat was hemmed with sympathy. She was a virtuous woman who dedicated all her days to a God-glorifying purpose: "She seeketh wool, and flax, . . . her candle goeth not out by night. She layeth her hands to the spindle, and her hands hold the distaff. She stretcheth out her hand to the poor; yea, she reacheth forth her hands to the needy" (Prov. 31:13, 18–20).

It was good for Dorcas to live for others. She kept herself too busy for self-pity, for the little jealousies that poison the mind and sometimes even the body. What does the average woman do with the time she has bought with modern appliances? She often has too much time to think and worry about herself, time to interfere in the affairs of others—usually with frustrating results. We hear much of nervous tension these days and of thwarted energy. The remedy psychiatrists frequently suggest is to keep the hands busy—preferably in doing for others. To abound in the work of the Lord, no matter how humble the task, is good for spiritual and physical health. Dorcas, contemplating the needs of others, minimized her own. That she was a pleasant woman, the best friend of many, and a saint among the disciples can be inferred from the effect her death had on all, including the apostle Peter.

Dorcas Was Good for Others

There were many poor in the days of Dorcas. Beggars were always in the streets begging alms at busy corners, at the gates of the wealthy (Luke 16:20), and at the gate of the temple (Acts 3:2). They were ignored, or despised and kicked about (James 2:6). It was not unusual to have many poor, but it was unusual to be much concerned about them. Jesus was concerned, for He made it plain that He came to preach the gospel to the poor (Luke 4:18). He advised, "When thou makest a feast, call the poor" (Luke 14:13). And He said, "Ye have the poor always with you" (Matt. 26:11) and "give to the poor" (Mark 10:21).

"Here I am, use me," prayed Dorcas, and she found great opportunity for benevolence right in her own city. Joppa, now called Yafa or Jaffa, was a busy seaport about thirty-five miles northwest of Jerusalem. It was on the Mediterranean seacoast just north of Philistia and originally belonged to the tribe of Dan (Josh. 19:46–48). This ancient city had a fascinating, legendary, and historical past. The town itself was built on an oblong, rocky ridge that extended into the sea to form a small, inadequate harbor. Insignificant and insecure as it was, it was Israel's only harbor and Jerusalem's one access to the Western world. Into its treacherous harbor had floated cedars for palaces, timber for both temples of the Lord (2 Chron. 2:16; Ezra 3:7), imports from Tarshish (Jer. 10:9), and the riches of Solomon (2 Chron. 9:21). It was the only harbor for the Western navy (1 Kings 10:22), and it was from here that Jonah had embarked for Spain. Boats were frequently upset, and lives were continually being lost. Consequently, there were always many seamen's widows and orphans in Joppa—perpetual poor in the busy little town on the rocky cape.

From the vantage point of her house, large enough to afford a commodious upper room, Dorcas had an excellent view of the beach and of the clumsy wooden ships as they idled in and near the port. Whenever she heard of a shipwreck, her compassionate heart went out to the forlorn. (There was work in the tanneries and soap factories for able men and prosperous businesses in luscious tropical fruit for the fortunate, but there was only the good will of a few for the widows and orphans.) Dorcas could see the poor as they picked up driftwood and rags on the beach. And she could see the anguished wives, eyes fixed helplessly on the horizon of the great sea for a sailor long overdue. Yes, Dorcas found great opportunity every day for almsdeeds, and she became the ministering angel of Joppa. The woman whose name became synonymous with charity was one of whom Jesus says, "Inasmuch as ye have done it unto one of the least of these my brethren, ye have done it unto me" (Matt. 25:40).

Dorcas Was Good for the Church

When Dorcas, in the midst of her many almsdeeds and good works, sickened and died, there was great grief and consternation in the church and community. They recalled how many an evening she was seen with a smile and a parcel, going down the streets of Joppa. Now they realized how wonderful she was, how they loved and needed her.

Peter, the inspired apostle, was in nearby Lydda where he had miraculously restored Aeneas. Two disciples were hastily dispatched to bring Peter for, in this time of severe loss, they needed his comfort and help. He responded immediately. When he came into the upper room where loving hands had laid Dorcas, he found mourners weeping inconsolably for the quiet woman they had come to love and need. There has never been a more touching and beautiful eulogy than that of the weeping widows as they showed Peter the coats and garments Dorcas had made for them.

Peter sensed the deep, earnest feeling of those who were bereft of a great benefactress and friend. With unflinching faith in the power of the risen Lord, Peter sent everyone from the room as he had seen Jesus do when He brought the daughter of Jairus back from death. After believing prayer, Peter performed the greatest miracle of his life when he said, "Tabitha, arise." (Acts 9:40). Seeing Peter, she sat up. Taking her by the hand, Peter presented her alive to the saints and widows.

In all of the Scripture we read of only eight people who were raised from the dead, one being Jesus who rose by His own mighty power. Dorcas, the seventh, was the first to rise in proof of the efficacy of the Resurrection. Imagine the amazement and joy of her friends! The mourner's dirge changed to songs of praise, and the news that Dorcas was alive again through the power of the Savior spread quickly. The disciples and saints were greatly strengthened in the faith, and "it was known throughout all Joppa; and many believed in the Lord" (Acts 9:42).

Terminating his work at Lydda, Peter stayed in Joppa for several months so that he might minister to the rapidly growing and flourishing church. And what did Dorcas do? She joined her loving, worn hands with the strong hands of the big fisherman in full and thankful service to her Lord. We may be sure that she once more picked up the ministry of the needle, testifying daily by word and deed to the grace of God.

The greatest service is always in doing the seemingly unimportant things in life (Matt. 25:4, 31–36). "Do not wait until some deed of greatness you may do; do not wait to shed your light afar, but brighten the corner where you are." A gift to the needy now and then will fall short of the mark of Dorcas, who was *full* of good works. It's absurd to say "be warmed and fed" to someone in need and then go our merry way and enjoy our abundance. Religion, pure and undefiled, is not only *saying* but, even more, *doing!*

> True worth is in being, not seeming,
> In doing, each day that goes by,
> Some little good, not in dreaming
> Of great things to do by and by,
> For what ever men say in their blindness
> And in spite of the fancies of youth,
> There is nothing so kingly as kindness
> And nothing so royal as truth.
> —Author Unknown

Suggestions for Discussion

1. Why did Dorcas find such great opportunity for benevolence?
2. Is there still a place for sewing circles and work parties in the church? Explain your view.

3. If you contribute regularly to a benevolent fund, is that fulfilling your Christian duty?
4. What are almsdeeds?
5. Are there opportunities for personal almsdeeds today? If so, make practical suggestions.
6. Can a person be too busy doing good?
7. What did the eulogy of Dorcas consist of?
8. How many people can you name who were raised from the dead?
9. What necessary virtues did Dorcas possess to be "full of almsdeeds and good works"?
10. Why do you think this story of Dorcas was recorded in all its detail?

If ye have judged me to be faithful to the Lord,
come into my house, and abide there.
—Acts 16:15

29

Lydia

Scripture Reading
Acts 16:9–15, 40

$\mathscr{P}$aul, a Jew of Tarsus and a Roman citizen, was the foremost apostle to the Gentiles. His Jewish name was Saul, but on his first missionary journey he became known as Paul. He was called by God to bring the gospel, and his commission included the special assignment to carry the Name above every name to the Gentiles.

The first church was distinctly Jewish, taking form in Jerusalem with its centralized council of elders and apostles. Charitable gifts were sent to Jerusalem where they were distributed to the poor. Supervision over the churches, missionaries, and ministers (Acts 16:4) was vested in the Jerusalem church, and appointments were made from there (Acts 11:22).

Paul was a minister at Antioch (where the disciples were first called Christians) when he was sent with Barnabas on his first missionary journey. Taking John Mark along as a helper, they sailed from Seleucia to the island of Cyprus. Spending about two years there, they also established churches at Perga in the Roman colony of Pamphylia, in Antioch, in Pisidia, in Derbe, in Iconium, and in Lystra, and then returned to Antioch, the sending church.

The success of Paul's work among the Gentiles led, however, to controversy within the church, and Paul was recalled to Jerusalem to attend an ecclesiastical meeting (Acts 15). After much discussion about certain Jewish ceremonials, a decision was reached. The churches implicated were informed of the decision by both letter and personal deputation. Paul, Barnabas, and two others were delegated to Antioch, whence Paul and Silas continued to the north and west to visit established churches and to make what is known as Paul's second missionary journey. Led by the Spirit to Troas in western Asia Minor, Paul was informed in a vision that he must go to Macedonia (Acts 16:9–10). The baffling hindrances that had thwarted his plans for Asia were now understood by the apostle, and he realized that the Holy Spirit was calling him away from his native land to bring the gospel to Europe. Paul had been chosen to be an apostle to the Gentiles (Acts 9:15), and now he was told to pioneer a new continent and to conquer a new world for Christ. He answered the call of the Spirit with the eager and high resolve of "I am ready to preach the gospel to you . . . also" (Rom. 1:15).

Procuring passage on a ship, Paul sailed directly across the Aegean Sea to Neapolis, a seaport on the Macedonian coast. There he stepped ashore with his three companions, Silas, Timothy, and Luke. All four were passionately eager to claim all of Europe for Christ. Yet that conquest of Europe had an unpretentious beginning, for it started at a riverside with one convert—a woman named Lydia.

The Businesswoman

In a day when men ruled with a ruthless hand and women had few rights even over their own children, Lydia was successful in the business world. In sacred history she is prominent because she was the first European convert and her family was the nucleus of the Christian church at Philippi.

The first thing Luke tells us about Lydia is that she was a "seller of purple." She knew her product well, for she was a native of Thyatira in Asia Minor. The Tyrian women were skilled in procuring the precious dyes from the veins of the *murex*, and the waters of the nearby Hermus river were especially good for bringing out the brilliant hues in the textiles. There were no colors as gorgeous as the crimsons and purples of Thyatira. A woman as enterprising as Lydia surely belonged to the Guild of Dyers of this ancient city. Lydia knew the secrets of the Tyrian tint that made the rich reds and purples for the clothing of royalty and the hangings for the temples of the goddess Diana.

Situated on a river and near the sea, the Lydian market enjoyed a wide and valuable trade with the entire Greco-Roman world. Lydia, with her keen foresight and business acumen, moved to Philippi, the principal city of Macedonia, where she found a ready market for her expensive textiles. No doubt she did a thriving business with the Jews in Philippi, for the enterprising Jews were to be found wherever there was a Roman colony. Did she sell them blue, purple, and scarlet for the temple draperies or for the vestments of the many priests of Jerusalem? Did they bargain with her for bolts of purple silk and linen to sell to the wealthy and to those who sit in king's houses?

We infer that Lydia was a widow who courageously and capably carried on her husband's trade for the sake of her children. Many women do not choose a business career for their own satisfaction but, for the sake of their children, will say, "I can do all things through Christ which strengtheneth me" (Phil. 4:13). And Lydia managed both her family and business well. In an age when women were held to be inferior, she successfully took her place beside men in business. Her sagacity and shrewdness were recognized. She had a personal charm that drew people to her and a sincerity that made them trust her. We like to think that she advertised her materials by wearing them herself and that she wore them beautifully, with royal grace and dignity.

Philippi, where Lydia lived, was called the city of fountains. It was named after Philip of Macedon, who founded it as well as exploiting its riches. Philippi is best known for a famous and decisive battle, for here, in 42 B.C., the legions of Anthony and young Octavius won a brilliant victory over Brutus and Cassius, who had assassinated Caesar. Octavius became the first Roman Emperor, the Augustus under whose rule the Roman empire enjoyed the blessings of a long period of peace. He reorganized government, commerce and industry were developed, a postal service came into being, and the great system of Roman roads was planned and built. (The Appian Way was the first of the great highways uniting the mighty Roman Empire.) Many modern roads are laid out on these routes, and some of the old bridges are still in use. In the ruins of ancient Philippi, archeologists have found the paved streets and squares still intact. At the western exit of the city, there was a great colonial archway that spanned the Via Egnatia, the highway that crossed the Gangites River (Angista, today), where Paul met Lydia on that Sabbath day some fifteen years after the crucifixion of Christ. Great were the glories of Philippi, a colony of the mighty Roman Empire, but greater than all was the event of the conversion of Lydia on the banks of the swift flowing river by the city wall.

The Believer

Long journeys such as Paul took, either by sea or land, presented no serious difficulty in those days. Roman roads were the best the Western world ever had until railways began to be built in the nineteenth century. Leaving the seaport, Paul and his friends, as they traveled the ten miles north and west through the wild Pangean mountain range to Philippi, were thankful for the safety of the roads. The Via Egnatia was policed by foot soldiers and prancing Roman cavalry. The well-maintained roads were equipped with halting places for changes of horses, and hostelries where people could rest and buy food. Conveniently, there was no language barrier, for Greek was used everywhere.

It was with good reason that Paul had chosen to go to Philippi.

He confidently expected to contact many Jews there. He had preached to multitudes of them in their own synagogues in Asia Minor (Acts 14:1). Why should it not be so in Philippi?

Eager and zealous to answer the call, "Come over . . . and help us" (Acts 16:9), the four men descended to the plains. What an impressive moment when they first sighted the Roman city! From the highway, noisy with clanging soldiery and racy chariots, they gazed at a modern Roman colony. They had glimpses of the forum, elaborate public buildings, and huge arcades set all together like a giant ornament in a lush and colorful landscape. Yes, travel was easy and pleasant. Did Luke muse on the prophetic words, "And a highway shall be there . . . the redeemed shall walk there" (Isa. 35:8–9)? Did Paul speak of the Via Dolorosa, of the One who died that He might become the highway to heaven?

But in the city they met no Macedonians asking for the gospel. They searched but found no synagogues among the pagan temples. Perhaps it was in the busy stalls of the market that they heard of a small *proseuche,* or prayer meeting place, just outside of the city by the Gangites River where Jewish people met on the Sabbath. There Paul, as was his custom, sought his own people. Was it disappointing to Paul, Luke, Timothy, and Silas to find only a few women there? Did Paul's message lack eloquence because it was preached in the shade of a few trees? Were not the groves God's first temples?

And "we sat down, and spake unto the women" (Acts 16:13), wrote Luke. One of the women was Lydia, the seller of purple. Though John Calvin says that she was Jewish, we are inclined to accept the version of others who say that she was a proselyte. She was brought up in the province of Lydia, which was known for its worship of the Great Diana. In her search for truth, she had been converted to Judaism. Lydia was earnest and faithful and took her family with her to prayer meetings. Many in her position would have found it more profitable, for business reasons, to join the large city church, even if it might mean toning down religious convictions. Some prefer to affiliate with a large church for social reasons, others because financial obligations are greater in a small church.

Lydia was not too proud to join a small group. Here, in service and prayer to God, she found blessing, renewed strength, and new hope for the future.

Paul told the women what had happened in Judea—the Messiah had come to be the Way, the Truth, and the Light to the Father. Lydia listened, spellbound, as Paul spoke eloquently, sincerely, and with a holy passion for souls. It was evident to Lydia that Paul was not ashamed of the cross of Christ—that he gloried in it. And the Lord opened her heart (Acts 16:14), and she believed when Paul spoke of the "Christ crucified, unto the Jews a stumblingblock, and unto the Greeks foolishness; but unto them which are called . . . the power of God, and the wisdom of God" (1 Cor. 1:23–24).

We who sit in the pews today should see in our ministers the spirit of Paul, for whom to live was Christ—his humility, sincerity, and consuming passion for souls (Phil. 1:21). Like Lydia, we must "attend unto the things spoken"—at worship services, at Bible studies, and at prayer meetings—and the Lord will open our hearts, for if we truly seek Him we will surely find Him.

The Builder

"I will build my church" at Philippi, said the Christ. And the same day that Lydia was converted she became His coworker to show forth the praises of Him who had called her "out of darkness into his marvelous light" (1 Peter 2:9). How did she begin? By being baptized with her household—including her children and servants. So, in one wonderful hour her family on earth became a family for heaven! Mothers, God has called you as you are, to serve Him where you are! Have you brought your family to Christ? *Yours* is that *priceless* privilege.

The fruits of the Spirit, of the opened heart, were immediately evident in other ways, also. Why did Lydia not have to be urged to witness for Christ, to attend the church, to be generous, and to show hospitality? Because she was spiritually alive! She begged to be of service. "If you have judged me to be faithful," she pleaded, "come to my house and make it your home." Her alabaster box and precious ointment became her home and hospitality, poured generously on the needy and the stranger. We hear again the echo of the Savior's voice, "She hath wrought a good work upon me" (Matt. 26:10).

Paul and his companions accepted her generous hospitality for many days. Lydia's family became the nucleus of the European church and her home a place of blessing for many. Who knows how many neighbors and friends Lydia welcomed into her home to meet Paul?

In Philippi, Paul experienced his first persecution, and Lydia began to realize what it might cost to live for Christ (Phil. 1:29). A true friend and courageous woman, she did not hesitate to show him kindness (Acts 16:40), even though it might seriously affect her business and personal safety (Acts 16:19–22). Paul and Silas left Philippi, but Luke and Timothy remained for a time. The church grew rapidly so that, in a short time, it could have its own bishops and deacons (Phil. 1:1). Lydia's hospitality and zeal remained a shining example for the rest of the church. When Paul visited the church later he could also say of Lydia, "For we are laborers together with God: . . . I have laid the foundation, and another buildeth thereon" (1 Cor. 3:9–10). Writing to the Philippians from Rome, Paul praised their love, thanked them for the gifts they had sent to him, and said, "I thank my God upon every remembrance of you" (Phil. 1:3).

Did Lydia, taking the torch from Paul, shine as a light "in the world; holding forth the word of life" (Phil. 2:15–16)? Jesus said, "Unto the angel of the church of Ephesus write; . . . I know thy works" (Rev. 2:1–2), "and charity, and service, and faith" (Rev. 2:19). "He that overcometh . . . to him will I give power" (Rev. 2:26).

"I will build my church" in Europe, in Asia, in Africa, in America . . .

Suggestions for Discussion

1. For a better understanding of the story of Lydia and the church to which she belonged, read the epistle to the Philippians.

2. What did Roman culture contribute to the spread of the gospel?

3. How did Lydia find Christ?

4. In what ways did the Holy Spirit operate in the heart of Lydia?

5. How were the fruits of the Spirit evident in Lydia's life?

6. What do we learn of the importance of the family in the building of the kingdom of God?

7. Can you name any other members of the church at Philippi? See Acts 16 and Philippians 4:2–3.

8. Cite the advantages of belonging to a small church.

9. Where will Christ build His church (Matt. 13:38; 28:19; Rev. 7:9)?

Unto whom not only I give thanks, but also all the churches of the Gentiles.
—Romans 16:4

30

Priscilla

Scripture Reading
Acts 18; Romans 16:3–5;
1 Corinthians 16:19; 2 Timothy 4:19

*M*any an inspiring line has been penned about friendship—its qualities and its values, how to attain it and how to preserve it. Some rather cynically suggest that there are no *real* friends—the kind who are loyal to others in all the vicissitudes of life. Many believe that, like the prodigal son, we all have many fair-weather friends and that friendship is basically selfish. But friendship, as Christ taught it, seeks nothing and gives all.

True friendship is a rare and beautiful thing. A friend is defined as one who is attached to another by esteem, respect, and affection. We have been created as social beings, and everyone needs a friend—someone who is sympathetic, understanding, and loyal. Real friends can be trusted to do good, or they are not friends at all. The Bible tells us that a friend loves at all times and that friendship has the quality of intimacy (John 15:15).

In the Bible, we learn about friendships that were short-lived, untrue, and unsympathetic. God's record also reveals beautiful friendships like those of Abraham, the friend of God; of David and Jonathan; and of the friend who sticks closer than a brother. Friendship is more than goodwill, harmony, and practical kindness. It is a spiritual thing, a melody that should grow so sweet and steady and loyal that it will last a lifetime. There is no more beautiful picture of Christian fellowship to be found anywhere than that of Priscilla, Aquila, and the apostle Paul. For human friendship, like all that is good and wonderful in human life, attains its acme when it has fellowship with God in common, and while the friends constantly labor together for the glory of the Friend of Sinners. Greater friendship—"greater love hath no man than this, that a man lay down his life for his friends" (John 15:13).

Priscilla's Wonderful Loyalty

Paul's friend, Priscilla, was a remarkable woman. She was one of the most prominent women in the New Testament church—perhaps the most influential of them all. Lydia was a pillar of the church at Philippi, but Priscilla was actively engaged in promoting the cause of Christ in Corinth, Ephesus, and Rome—three of the most important cities in the Roman Empire. Paul enlarges upon the scope of her Christian service by writing that *all* the churches of the Gentiles owed much to her (Rom. 16:4). Paul was grateful to Priscilla for many things. He could say, "I thank my God always on your behalf," and by calling her Prisca tells us that she was a much loved and intimate friend (2 Tim. 4:19).

Though Priscilla and her husband labored together in the gospel, in three out of the five times they are mentioned she is named first, making it evident that she was the more energetic of the two—an outstanding and consecrated woman. Paul's admiration for her and the place of leadership she occupied in the early church give an answer to the often discussed problem of the woman's place (must she keep silent?) in the work of the church. May God give us many Priscas, beloved "messengers of the churches, and the glory of Christ" (2 Cor. 8:23) who are "steadfast, unmovable, always abounding in the work of the Lord" (1 Cor. 15:58).

Priscilla was a distinctly Roman name meaning old, or of *ancient blood*. Some suggest that Priscilla herself was of noble birth, a distinguished and well-educated Italian woman who married Aquila, a rich Jew of Pontus. We can be sure that she was distinguished for her influence in the early church, for we read in secular history that "by the holy Prisca, the gospel is preached." Churches and monuments have been dedicated to her, and a memorial has been raised to her remembrance in the Sacred Word.

In all the references to Priscilla, no quality of character is more conspicuous than her wonderful loyalty to her husband, to her friend Paul, to the church, and to the Lord Jesus Christ. Her husband moved often—from Pontus to Rome, then to Corinth, next to Ephesus, once again to Rome, and then back to Ephesus. Priscilla loyally went with him everywhere; they were so compatible that, in every instance, they are named together.

Aquila was a Jew of Pontus (a land on the shores of the Black Sea), where there was a large colony of Jews. He had moved to Rome and, considering that he appears to have been fairly wealthy, we infer that it was with an eye for business that he moved to Rome, the largest city in the world. There he prospered at his tent-making trade, and it is quite possible that he had a home large enough to be used later as a church.

There came a sudden change in his fortunes, however, when Emperor Claudius unjustly evicted all Jews from Rome. There were many Jews in this cosmopolitan city, and it is quite certain that some were Christians. Many believe the historian who says that this cruel edict was occasioned by frequent riots, or attacks of unbelieving Jews upon the Christian Jews, similar to those in Jerusalem, Thessalonica, Ephesus, and elsewhere. It is possible that

Priscilla and Aquila were already acquainted with Christianity when they came to Corinth as exiles, in search of a home and a living.

Paul's Enduring Friend

Corinth, where they went into business once again, was a renowned trading and packing center. There the wares of the Orient met those of Europe. Built on an isthmus between the Adriatic and Aegean Seas, it was one of the most beautiful cities in the ancient world. Great fortresses and majestic temples towered on the rocky heights above it. The sides of the hills were beautifully terraced and dotted with palaces of wealthy merchants of many nations who lived there. According to modern archeologists who followed the steps of St. Paul to Corinth, the city was grand and well constructed with broad pavements and an ingenious system of mains through which fresh mountain water flowed continuously to the markets of perishable foods and meats. It was to the Christians in Corinth that Paul wrote, "Whatsoever is sold in the shambles, that eat" (1 Cor. 10:25).

But cultured and luxurious Corinth was a citadel of sin. It was notorious for its vices, its love of pleasure, its superstition, and its intemperance. It came to symbolize wealth, expensive living, and night life to the extent that the expression "to Corinthianize" came into vogue, or as the modern Greek still says, with a shrug, "not every one can sail to Corinth." It became common to say of an immoral person, "He is a Corinthian." In this city Paul founded a congregation that was at once his pride and despair (1 and 2 Corinthians).

Paul had come from Athens, where he had talked in the Agora to anyone who would listen. But they did not give him much of a hearing, for the thinkers of the day sought to perpetuate the spirit of their illustrious predecessors, Socrates, Plato, and Aristotle. Paul's "spirit was stirred in him" (Acts 17:16) when he gazed up at the great Parthenon with the huge gold and ivory statue of the goddess

Athena and "he saw the city wholly given to idolatry" (Acts 17:16). When giving his speech on the Areopagus he was cut short, and he left Athens for Corinth.

Highly educated for professional work, Paul had suffered the loss of all things "for the excellency of the knowledge of Christ Jesus" (Phil. 3:8). So he had fallen back on his avocation, tent making (a good trade in those days), to earn a living. In Corinth Paul found employment with Aquila, the tent maker. Paul, Aquila, and his wife Priscilla, with the common bond of trade, race, and interests, soon became fast friends. Priscilla, energetic and intelligent, made a comfortable and cheerful home for Paul. It is certain that, as the men busily stitched away day after day, Paul talked persuasively of Jesus and His great salvation. Aquila, doubtless well versed in the Scriptures, listened with growing conviction. Priscilla, working along with them, perhaps cutting out the hard goats-hair cloth to be sewn, listened with intense interest to the words of eternal life. Soon their friendship was cemented with the bonds of the love of Christ, and now there were three who looked upon Corinth as a great mission field.

There were many Jews in the city, and together the three friends attended the large synagogue where Paul preached Christ cruci-fied. How they rejoiced when one and then another of their Jewish brethren believed, and what a day of prayer and praise when Crispus, the *ruler* of the synagogue, and his family accepted Jesus! Paul spent about two years in Corinth, enjoying the blessed fellowship and able assistance of Priscilla in the gospel ministry. Part of this time he lived with Justus, a Greek proselyte, perhaps to insure the safety and prosperity of his good friends, Priscilla and her husband, per-haps to make more contacts with the Gentiles. How thrilled Priscilla must have been with the apostle when many Greeks and Corinthians were "called to be saints."

⅔   ⅔   ⅔

Leaving Timothy and Silas to carry on the work, Paul left for Jerusalem (Acts 18:5, 18). Priscilla and her husband sailed with him from Corinth as far as Ephesus on the opposite side of the sea. During a brief visit, Paul and his helpers laid the foundation for the church at Ephesus, and it assembled in the home of Priscilla (1 Cor. 16:19). Priscilla's home was devout and peaceful, a place to which Christians gladly came and where they shared great spiritual experiences. Priscilla was no halfway or part-time Christian. She was consistently energetic and loyal in the work of the Lord all her life long.

Priscilla was an amazing woman. Besides keeping a large and pleasant home, working at tent making with her husband, performing the duties involved with keeping the church in her home, and entertaining strangers, she found time to be a thorough student of the Scriptures. A highly intelligent woman, she had been a serious student of Paul while he lodged at her home. The profound concepts of the kingdom had become clear to her, and she so perfectly understood the way of God that she was able to instruct Apollos, who himself was mighty in the Scriptures (Acts 18:24–26). Apollos, a graduate of the renowned schools of Alexandria in Egypt, was the most eloquent and popular speaker in the early church. Yet he so respected the intelligence and piety of Priscilla, the tent maker, that he gladly received instruction from her. Priscilla was wise enough to know that the limited knowledge of the gifted Apollos could do irreparable harm to the infant church. She entertained Apollos in her home while she "expounded unto him the way of God more perfectly" (Acts 18:26).

Priscilla stayed in Ephesus for a long time. Whenever Paul came to Ephesus we can be sure that he stayed with Priscilla and Aquila, and that they shared his cares and labors. Together they praised the glory of His grace, wherein He had accepted the Ephesians in His beloved Son (Eph. 1:6).

⁂   ⁂   ⁂

After the death of Claudius and when Nero came into power, Priscilla and her husband returned to Rome. We read (Rom. 16:3–5) that there, too, they gathered the church into their home. Was Priscilla among the Christians in Rome who met and comforted the apostle Paul when he was brought a prisoner in chains to Caesar? It could well be. It might have been at the apostle's suggestion that Priscilla moved once again to Ephesus where Timothy was ministering to the church. There, perhaps now an elderly woman mellow and rich with tremendous spiritual experiences, she was of inestimable help to young Pastor Timothy. Impressed with the imminence of his death when writing to Timothy, Paul greets, before all others, his beloved and faithful colaborers in the gospel, Prisca and Aquila (2 Tim. 4:19).

Priscilla, energetic, loyal, and learned in Christian wisdom, was not afraid to sacrifice for the cause of Christ. She lived in a day of great prejudice and opposition to the Christ of the Christian church. She confessed Christ in a day when Christians faced great persecution. But Priscilla was not afraid, even if her life was in danger (Rom. 16:3–4). As for her friend Paul, so it was for her—to live was Christ and to die could be but gain. Streams of blessing flowed from the heart and home of Priscilla wherever she lived—in Rome, in Corinth, or in Ephesus. By her godly example, she continues to bless and serve the church today.

According to tradition, Priscilla died a martyr's death. We prefer to think that she moved from Ephesus to her heavenly home and that, shining like the stars (Dan. 12:3), she stepped through its portals with her willing hands full of jewels for the diadem of the King of Kings—and that, having been faithful and loyal to the end, she was given to eat of the tree of life, which is in the midst of the paradise of God (Rev. 2:7).

Suggestions for Discussion

1. Take time to read the two letters to the Corinthians and the one to the Ephesians. You will learn much about the characters and the problems of the people with whom Priscilla worked and prayed and worshiped.

2. Where or when do you suppose Priscilla risked her life for Paul (Acts 18:12; 19:29–30)?

3. Why did the Jews stir up trouble for Paul wherever he established churches?

4. Some say that it is harder to win the Corinthian type of person for Christ than the Athenian type. What do you think?

5. Priscilla was a remarkable, unusually fine, and gifted woman. Explain how her humility, industry, loyalty, intelligence, friendship, and courage were manifested.

6. Where and how is our Christian loyalty evident today?

7. Paul was beheaded outside Rome; Peter was crucified upside down at Rome; the apostle John (whom Priscilla knew, for he was also a minister at Ephesus) was banished for his testimony for Jesus Christ. Deprived of these great leaders, how did the church go on?

8. What kind of church work can women do today?

Train up a child in the way he should go: and when he is old, he will not depart from it.
—Proverbs 22:6

31

ℒois and ℰunice

Scripture Reading
Acts 16:1–5; 2 Timothy 1:1–5

𝒲e often hear about great men—noted inventors and scientists, renowned authors and artists, prominent men in church and state, eminent theologians, valiant soldiers, proud dictators, and able presidents. History will always know, by name, such famous men as Moses, Paul, Caesar Augustus, Napoleon, Michelangelo, and St. Augustine.

In Scripture, we do not hear about great women as often as we do great men. More often it is good women that we hear about. Citing Sarah as an example, Peter writes that in the old times the holy women adorned themselves with "the ornament of a meek and quiet spirit, which is in the sight of God of great price" (1 Peter 3:4). Paul tells the women of the New Testament that they should lift up holy hands to pray. He states that women should "adorn themselves in modest apparel, with shamefacedness and sobriety; not with braided hair, or gold, or pearls, or costly array; but (which becometh women professing godliness) with good works" (1 Tim. 2:9–10). The heroines that shall be forever remembered are the Marys, Sarahs, Jochebeds, and Rachels—the good women who lived by faith.

It is well to remember, too, that behind nearly every great man there was a good mother who, in the quiet of the home and the intimate family circle, taught and guided, implanting high ideals and moral principles, and in doing so molded character for usefulness and eventual greatness. Who can estimate the power and influence of a good mother? In God's perfect plan, Samuel needed a Hannah, Moses a Jochebed, John the Baptist an Elisabeth, and St. Augustine a Monica.

Many an illustrious son has honored his mother by attributing much of his success to the training given him by his mother. John Quincy Adams said of his mother, "From her I derived whatever instruction (religious especially, and moral) has pervaded a long life . . . whatever imperfection there has been . . . the fault is mine, not hers." George Washington, Henry Clay—great men in the history of our country—Napoleon, the Englishman Cromwell, and Thomas Grey all had wonderful mothers. The poet William Cowper paid this tribute:

> I do not boast that I derive my birth
> From loins enthroned or rulers of the earth.
> But higher still my proud pretensions rise,
> The child of parents passed into the skies.

The paramount testimony is that of St. Augustine to his mother Monica, "The mother in female garb with masculine faith." He praises God for her motherly love, saintly character, Christian piety, and persistence in prayer for his salvation. After many years of living in sin, Augustine was converted. Devoting his life to God, he prayed, "O Lord, I am Thy servant and the son of Thy handmaid. . . ."

An equally noble example of a great son and a good mother is found in the story of Timothy, his mother Eunice, and his grandmother Lois. Eunice represents Christian motherhood at its best. Her unfeigned faith, prayers, and labors of love produced, though unawares, one of the greatest leaders in the Christian church.

Good Mother and Pious Grandmother

Lois the grandmother and Eunice the mother, with her son Timothy, lived together in Lystra, a city in Lycaonia. Though they were Jewish, they lived among a people who worshiped the gods of the Greeks. At the most there were only a few Jewish families in Lystra (perhaps only this one family), for we do not read of a synagogue or even a small prayer meeting place there. We wonder why such godly Jewish women went to live in this heathen city. Then we read that Eunice married a Greek and conclude that Lois went to live with Eunice and her husband in this city of Asia Minor. Here Timothy was born to Eunice and her Grecian husband, and he was likely their only child. It is believed that Eunice's husband remained Greek—that is, remained a heathen, never even becoming a Jewish proselyte.

Eunice was a faithful wife, a virtuous woman, whose price was "far above rubies . . . the heart of her husband doth safely trust in her" (Prov. 31:10–11). She certainly wanted her son to be admitted by circumcision into God's ancient covenant, but doubtless his heathen father would not consent to it. And so Timothy was more Greek than Jewish until, when he was a young man, Paul (Acts 16:3) took and circumcised him before taking him along to visit the churches. A wise and devout Israelite, Eunice knew that circumcision was but a sign and that true religion was a matter of the heart. The father might forbid the Jewish rite, but he could not prevent the mother from bringing up their child in the faith of Israel.

Though the early training of a Jewish child devolved upon the father, the first training would be by the mother. Eunice accepted the law as a personal and sacred duty: "Hear therefore, O Israel . . .

these words . . . thou shalt teach them diligently unto thy children, and shalt talk of them when thou sittest in thine house, and when thou walkest by the way, and when thou liest down, and when thou risest up" (Deut. 6:3, 6–7). With all earnestness and diligence, Eunice fulfilled her sacred trust, for when Timothy was a man Paul wrote to him, "Continue thou in the things which thou hast learned . . . knowing of whom thou hast learned them" (2 Tim. 3:14).

It is believed that Eunice's husband died when Timothy was a young boy and that she was already a widow when Paul visited Lystra for the first time (Acts 14:6–7). As a young widow, she likely had to earn a living for her family. There were many things a widow could work at in her day. She could have been a seamstress, a tent maker, or a weaver of cloth. Did she work in the dye or textile business, or work in the marketplace? Did she perhaps teach, as did Priscilla? Whatever Eunice did, we conclude that she was away from her home much of the time because of the noticeable part Lois took in the training of Timothy.

❧   ❧   ❧

Timothy must have been repeating small portions of Scripture and learning little prayers early, for Paul recalled that Timothy had known the Scriptures (2 Tim. 3:15) since he was small. Jewish children were always fascinated by the shiny metal phylacteries (*mesusahs,* in which the name of God was written ten times) fastened on the doorposts, and they reached with childish curiosity for the phylacteries on their father's forehead. But in a home such as Timothy's there would be no phylacteries. There would be no holy example or the religious companionship of a father. There was no synagogue in Lystra where Timothy could go every Sabbath and twice in the week to hear the prophets read, no impressive symbols and services to watch, no inspiring feast days to keep. And there were few, if any, of his kind to play with. It might well have been that every boy in Timothy's neighborhood lived in a home in which Jupiter and Mercurius were worshiped. But there was one influence for good in Timothy's life, and it was the most powerful of all—the constant, prayerful influence of "mothers in Israel," that of his good mother and pious grandmother. His home was a happy, sacred place. He found love there in abundance, along with security and peace. There, he was made spiritually strong for life, for he was daily "nourished up in the words of faith and of good doctrine" (1 Tim. 4:6).

Of the Same Mind and Faith

Lois and Eunice were of the same mind and faith. They held the same ideals. They both feared God, awaited the Messiah, and adored little Timothy. Grandmother Lois, because she was older, understood even better than mother Eunice the necessity of sound religious and moral training. She knew from years of observation that Proverbs 22:6 was no pretty platitude: "Train up a child in the way he should go: and when he is old, he will not depart from it." A child's life was something peculiarly holy to these good women, and their duty of filling it with thoughts of God was specially sacred.

Lois and Eunice knew full well the implications of a broken home and the perils of a heathen atmosphere. Every boy needs a father that he may learn manliness and courage, and how to compete and succeed in the world from which he must wrest a living. It is father whose physical strength a boy admires and who encourages his son to develop a rugged constitution. Eunice must have felt her inadequacy. She could not be both a father and a mother to her son. How earnestly she must have prayed for divine help; how conscientiously she guided Timothy and taught him all she knew. Eunice and Lois were wise women who knew how to speak a word in season and how to make God wonderful and real to a boy.

We learn from the letters of Paul to Timothy that the latter was a good mother's son, having imbibed qualities of tenderness, love, and tears. He was not physically strong, for Paul was concerned about Timothy's "often infirmities" (1 Tim. 5:23). But Paul cheers Timothy when he writes that "bodily exercise profiteth little: but godliness is profitable unto all things, having promise of the life that now is, and of that which is to come" (1 Tim. 4:8).

Good Teachers

By the time that Timothy was five years old, he knew the Hebrew alphabet and was learning to read the Scriptures. There was no Jewish school in Lystra (if there was no synagogue) where he could continue his formal education. Perhaps Eunice and Lois accepted the full responsibility of Timothy's education. They were imbued with all the requirements of good Jewish teachers. They were patient and honest (never making promises that they could not keep), and their object was moral training as well as intellectual training. Adhering to the prescribed procedure, they would first teach portions of Leviticus, then the rest of the Pentateuch, the Psalms, and the Prophets. Women so well versed in the Scriptures might have had the whole of the Old Testament in their home—perhaps even little parchments made especially for little children.

The lessons were not only taught, but lived. Personal testimony about the love and grace of God was not strange to the ears of Timothy. There was no friction in the home because grandmother lived there, for Lois was wanted, needed, and loved. The everyday lives of Eunice and Lois were testimonies to their faith in God— holy epistles to be read by all people, but first and most intimately by Timothy. They influenced him more than anything else.

※   ※   ※

When Timothy was only a boy the apostle Paul visited Lystra. Perhaps Timothy was jostled in the excited mob that had impetuously tried to worship Paul after he healed a disabled man there (Acts 14:6–12)—the mob that had as senselessly turned on Paul to stone him. It could have been Lois and Eunice who washed Paul's wounds and that very evening might have heard from Paul the story of Jesus. They were converted from Judaism to Christianity and were further instructed in the Way when Paul came to Lystra the second time.

When Paul later visited the cities of Lycaonia, he heard good reports everywhere of the exemplary conduct of young Timothy. Knowing the firmness of Timothy's convictions, Timothy being a third generation believer of unfeigned faith, Paul decided to take him along as a helper on his missionary journeys. This unfeigned faith was a faith of conviction—a faith in the risen Lord and the hope of eternal life so sure that it could endure persecution, the loss of all things, even death itself for the sake of Christ. It was this unfeigned faith that Eunice the mother and Lois the grandmother had passed down as a precious heirloom to their beloved Timothy. It was this unfeigned faith that allowed Eunice gladly to give her only son to the furtherance of the gospel, even though it might mean hardship, trial, and even martyrdom. She must eagerly have awaited news from him and been constant in prayer for his work and well-being. Some say that she went to live with him in Ephesus when he was a bishop there, but this, though possible, is only conjecture.

Timothy became great because his mother was faithful to the high calling of Christian motherhood. Because she considered it her sacred duty to bring her son up in the fear and admonition of the Lord, Timothy became the "man of God" (1 Tim. 6:11) who was sent by Paul to accomplish the most difficult tasks (for example, 1 Cor. 4:17ff.). Called the beloved spiritual son of Paul (2 Tim. 1:2; 2:1), he was endowed with the Spirit of God. He became an evangelist and a good minister of Jesus Christ (1 Tim. 4:6; 2 Tim. 4:5).

Suggestions for Discussion

1. Is it good for children to have both a mother and a grandmother to supervise and bring them up?
2. Read 1 and 2 Timothy and note the references to Timothy's early training and the influence of his mother and grandmother.

3. What is unfeigned faith (2 Tim. 1:5)? How is faith imparted?
4. How important is home training today?
5. What does each parent normally contribute to the development of children?
6. Discuss the kinds of activities that our children engage in day to day. How much time is involved, and how much time is left for religious training? How can we achieve a proper balance?

Selected Bibliography

Bible Dictionaries

Davis, John B., and Henry S. Gebman. *The Westminster Dictionary of the Bible.* Philadelphia: Westminster, 1944.

Orr, James. *International Standard Bible Encyclopedia.* Grand Rapids: Eerdmans, 1956.

Bible Commentaries

Barnes, Albert. *Notes on the Old and New Testaments.* Grand Rapids: Baker, 1949.

———. *Barnes' Notes on the New Testament.* Grand Rapids: Kregel, 1962.

Calvin, John. *Commentaries on the Bible.* Grand Rapids: Eerdmans, 1949.

Jamieson, Robert, A. R. Fausett, and David Brown. *Commentary on the Whole Bible.* Grand Rapids: Zondervan, 1934.

Nicoll, W. Robertson, ed. *The Expositor's Bible.* Grand Rapids: Eerdmans, 1947.

Books on Bible Characters

Deen, Edith. *All the Women of the Bible.* New York: Harper and Brothers, 1955.

Kuyper, Abraham. *Women of the New Testament.* Grand Rapids: Zondervan, 1933.

———. *Women of the Old Testament.* Grand Rapids: Zondervan, 1934.

Matheson, George. *Portraits of Bible Women.* Grand Rapids: Kregel, 1986.

Powell, Ivor. *Bible Cameos.* Grand Rapids: Kregel, 1985.

———. *Bible Highways.* Grand Rapids: Kregel, 1985.

———. *Bible Pinnacles.* Grand Rapids: Kregel, 1985.

———. *Bible Treasures.* Grand Rapids: Kregel, 1985.

Whyte, Alexander. *Bible Characters from the Old and New Testaments.* Grand Rapids: Kregel, 1990.

The Spiritual Woman
Ten Principles of Spirituality and the Women Who Have Lived Them
by Lewis and Betty Drummond
0-8254-2469-0

> "I most heartily recommend this book to all women, and men also. Read it, take the steps suggested, and find true holiness and maturity in the Lord."
> —Ruth Bell Graham

This collection of biographies and devotional reflections illustrates ten steps that women can take to attain deeper spirituality and greater closeness to God. The stories of these women's struggles and victories will challenge and encourage the reader on her quest to be a Spirit-led woman of God.

Kay Arthur	"Growing in God"
Vonetta Bright	"Sharing God"
Jill Briscoe	"Knowing God"
Evelyn Christenson	"Talking with God"
Elisabeth Elliot Gren	"Loving God"
Martha Franks	"Exemplifying God"
Anne Graham Lotz	"Overflowing with God"
Henrietta Mears	"Serving God"
Jessie Penn-Lewis	"Abiding in God"
Amanda Smith	"Submitting to God"

Women of Awakenings
*The Historic Contribution of Women to
Revival Movements*
by Lewis and Betty Drummond
0-8254-2474-7

Lewis and Betty Drummond begin with
Deborah in the book of Judges and trace
the historic role of women in revivals
through the awakenings of the last three
centuries. Included are chapters on
Susannah Wesley, Evangeline Booth, Amy
Carmichael, Bertha Smith, and Ruth Bell
Graham.

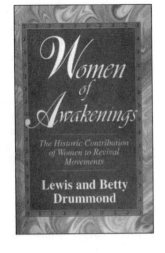

"These are ordinary women like you
and me who simply walked in faith. . . .
It is my prayer that God will use this book to revive you."
—*Kay Arthur*

"Books that model women of faith make a difference in an
upside-down culture. . . . This book helps."
—*Jill Briscoe*

"As I sincerely recommend this volume, I cannot help but
wonder that there would be more awakenings if there were
more men and women such as Lewis and Betty who would
encourage, instruct, guide, and liberate women as we seek to
develop our spiritual gifts and answer God's call in our lives."
—*Anne Graham Lotz*

"This book gives us not only the biblical and historical
evidence of God using women in past revivals, but the
possibility of God doing it again. What a timely and
encouraging book!"
—*Evelyn Christenson*

A Quiet Center
A Woman's Guide to Resting in God's Presence
Susan Sutton
0-8254-3662-1

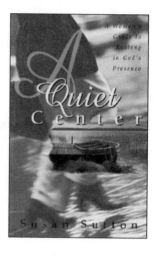

Daily chores pull in every direction—the boss is demanding; the laundry piles up; the phone keeps ringing; the kids need rides. And day after day your Bible sits on the end table by the bed, unopened.

This devotional is aimed at you,
the woman who
longs for peace in the midst of an
over-busy life.

Find a comfy chair. Let this refreshing guide show you how to still your soul before God, how to spend time alone with Him, and how to keep His restful presence within you throughout the day. Each chapter ends with a list of Scriptures and guidelines for meditation.

Find what God so wants to offer you—a dwelling place alone with Him . . . a quiet center.

A Woman's Guide to Keeping Promises
Fifty-Two Ways to Choose Happiness and Fulfillment
by Judith Rolfs
0-8254-3627-3

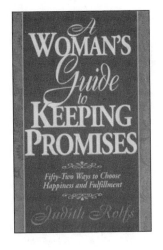

While the Christian men's movement has emphasized male responsibilities in society and the home, Judith Rolfs is deeply concerned that Christian women also find creative ways to deepen their spiritual lives and honor their commitments to God, themselves, and others. Some of the fifty-two chapters include:

> Deepening Friendships
> Respecting Your Mate
> Preventing Family Problems
> Keeping the Joy
> Releasing Creativity
> Surviving Your Husband's Life Crises
> Leading Others to Christ
> Aging with Grace
> Equipping Children
> Hearing God
> Being a Grandma

Her experiences as a Christian counselor, wife, and mother provide an insightful perspective on the challenges and opportunities of today's single women, wives, and mothers.